THE HUMAN ADVENTURE BEGINS ANEW. . . .

I looked around me. We were on the grounds of the National Aeronautics and Space Administration at Palmdale, California. To my right were Nichelle Nichols, Gene Roddenberry, Leonard Nimoy, George Takei, De Forest Kelley and Jimmy Doohan. The occasion was the Rollout of Shuttle Orbiter 101. . . .

Mr. John F. Yardley, the Associate Administrator, Office of Space Flight, NASA, called for the Rollout to begin. . . . Then it happened. The band leader moved his hands with an emphatic gesture and suddenly we were standing and shaking hands and embracing each other. *The space craft was approaching to the theme music from Star Trek*. The same chill ran down all our spines. . . . I felt myself close to tears and wasn't in the least embarrassed by it. Orbiter 101 was now directly in front of us. Who says there has to be a line between reality and fantasy? . . . Across the nose of the ship was the word "ENTERPRISE."

Star Trek liv

3 —

CHEKOV'S ENTERPRISE

Walter Koenig

A Personal Journal of the Making of Star Trek-The Motion Picture

PUBLISHED BY POCKET BOOKS NEW YORK

Panavision ™ is a trademark of Panavision, Inc.
Moviola ® is a registered trademark of Magnasync/Moviola
Corp.

Another *Original* publication of POCKET BOOKS

POCKET BOOKS, a Simon & Schuster division of
GULF & WESTERN CORPORATION
1230 Avenue of the Americas, New York, N.Y. 10020

ISBN: 0-671-83286-7

First Pocket Books printing March, 1980

10 9 8 7 6 5 4 3 2 1

POCKET and colophon are trademarks of Simon & Schuster.

Printed in the U.S.A.

DEDICATION

TO:

*Sarah and Isidore and Norm and Vera
for helping shape the first two decades*

AND TO: -

*Judy and Josh and Danielle
for all the rest*

ACKNOWLEDGMENTS

I wish to thank Ron Marx and Jack Danon, whose encouragement and support were instrumental in the writing of this book.

My gratitude as well to the cast, the crew, and everyone in all the offices at *Star Trek* and Paramount who made my four months on the motion picture such a memorable experience.

A very special thanks to Gene Roddenberry and Robert Wise for always being artists and gentlemen.

CHEK'ing-OUT KOENIG

Introduction by
HARLAN ELLISON

Of all the friends I've made during my eighteen years in Hollywood, only six or seven are actors. That isn't odd, despite the vast amount of time and work I've invested in writing for motion pictures and television. There are, of course, writers who become celebrity groupies; writers who either see a main chance in chumming it up with stars, or who gull themselves into believing that they are, themselves, stars; one frequently finds it easier to get writing assignments on the basis of whom one knows rather than how well one performs on the written page.

Blessedly, and I guess it's more because of my towering, arrogant conviction that *work* is the only cachet worthy of merit than any systemic nobility on my part, I've never been inclined to curry favor with the thespians just to promote my writing. Additionally, I have serious reservations about what it takes to want to be a "star" (as opposed to being an *actor*) . . . even as I suspect the nature of people who choose to be cops. But that's another, more questionable, infinitely more philosophical discussion, better saved for another time.

Suffice to say I am tainted with prejudice in that

area. So it takes a remarkable human being to penetrate my irrational barriers where actors are concerned.

Walter Koenig, who incidentally happens to make a part of his living as an actor, has been my friend for seventeen years.

The gentle sadness for those of you who have bought this, Walter's first book, is that you will probably never get to know him as a man, as a writer concerned with his craft, as a friend, as a kind and thoughtful human being fully decked out with all the warmth and chill and amusing personal idiosyncracies that make him an extraordinary individual.

From the evening in 1963 on the set of an "Alfred Hitchcock Hour" being filmed at Universal Studios, where we met, to this week when we worried about getting the missing comic character premiums needed to complete our sets of DC superheroes, the friendship between Koenig and Ellison has been no less wonky and stormy and rewarding than that between Gilgamesh and Inkidu. Thus it happily falls to me to introduce him. Not so much to introduce his log of the time spent working on the *Star Trek* motion picture, as to say a few words about him personally.

(Please understand: were the rigors of publishing, and the inflexible demands of pricing books within reach of a large readership, less stringent, I would ramble on at length about this singular personal diary. But only two pages were available for my maundering, and what the hell, you're paying to read Koenig, not Ellison, so the best I can hope to do is illuminate the man behind all the words. And properly so.)

As *Chekov's Enterprise* clearly demonstrates, there is a singular intellect at work in everything Walter undertakes. Whether it is adding dimensions to a stock tv series character coldbloodedly created to lure the Beatles-loving young viewers of the Sixties, writing a dark fantasy feature film for the tube, explaining over network talkshows the pain as well as the joy of being a "celebrity," writing a full-length novel, or raising two of the most astonishing children this side of *Village of the Damned*, Walter Koenig, is a *rara avis*, a man of depth and sensitivity and talent it makes one bewildered and pleased to know on day-to-day terms.

His record of the many months laboring in the cinematic vineyards is good solid reading. Not so much because it contains endless bits of minutiae about "show biz"—and God knows we've seen that kind of record before—but because it is one with all the worthy "confessional writing" of the past, whether Rousseau or Edward Abbey. It is a slice of a man's life, and its merit is not welded to the value of any single motion picture or great painting or political theory; its value lies in the worthiness of the man.

And while I have not the space to laud the smallest nook and cranny of the book you hold, I hope in this small space I have indicated the worthiness of the man who wrote the book.

You may know him as Walter Koenig, actor (and I pray you know that more readily than you know him as Chekov). I know him as friend; and it is my wish that these words introduce you to him as Walter Koenig, oh yeah, isn't he that writer?

HARLAN ELLISON
Los Angeles
August 2, 1979

PREFACE

SEPTEMBER 17, 1976: It was not a day like any other. For one thing it was 6:15 in the morning. Not even the Horta is up at that hour! I staggered into the bathroom and looked in the mirror. Was this the face that launched a thousand ships? Was this a face in a thousand at the launching of one ship? Grudgingly, I admitted to the latter.

By 7:25 A.M. I was ready to leave. Only one of the dogs was awake and he, in pursuit of a flea, ignored my departure. So much for fanfare and farewell.

I met De Forest Kelley, who plays Dr. Leonard "Bones" McCoy, at 7:40 A.M. and we drove the thirty-mile distance together. We had always gotten along well, but neither of us had had that obligatory first cup of coffee, and without it a discussion of Talosian hat size or the number of bumps on a Gorn would have been as overwhelming as a critique of Marcel Proust. We rode in silence.

I saw cows grazing on a hillside and watched as the morning brightened and the sky turned blue and asked myself if I really had this day in perspective. I worked at sorting my feelings. There was a fine line here between reality and fantasy, and I had to be on guard against crossing over. After all, we weren't on our way to a sound stage, we would not be presented with a script of colored pages, and yet, and yet . . . No! When

Ronald Colman played Othello in *Double Life* and
came to believe he *was* the Moor, he was *crazy*. It
had become looney-bin time, the funny farm follies.
Steady, Walter, steady. And yet . . .

A dull ache creased my frontal lobe. I was being
pounded by pondering, overdosing on cogitation. I
shut off my head and turned on the radio.

The music blared loudly and I felt the pain ebbing.
So much more comfortable to "dry out" on *what has
been* than to wring the truth from *what might be*.

I was snapping my fingers and singing along with the
music. De Forest looked at me strangely and inched
closer to the door on his side. I could tell he was
anxious for us to arrive at our destination.

The guard at the gate looked at us warily but let us
pass when he recognized De. I made a mental note to
stick close by my companion once we were on foot.
I didn't want to take the chance of going unidentified
and face arrest by the F.B.I. for spying.

We were ushered into a hospitality building and led
to the suite with the coffee. I drank gratefully while
exchanging pleasantries with members of our former
crew.

The minutes ticked by. The room was filling up.
Smoke grew thick, laughter increased, the activity level
heightened. The moment of truth was at hand. The
signal was given and we began to file out.

We crossed the plant yard and made for the portable
chairs erected for the occasion. Suddenly there were
reporters and photographers everywhere and they were
descending on *us*. I kept telling myself that this was
wrong. My grasp on reality was fragile at best, and all
this attention was beginning to pry loose my grip. I
was grateful that no one stopped. Undaunted, the men
with the cameras peddled backward, snapping, snapping, snapping.

We arrived at the viewing area and again I felt shaken; a row of chairs up front had been cordoned off exclusively for our benefit. As we approached, a dozen hands thrust forward seeking autographs. We signed, signed, signed.

Like a nun with her beads, over and over I vowed to myself humility; we were here as spectators, observers, just part of the thousand faces. I would not, like Ronald Colman, be seduced into believing that we really were a part of this, that somehow we were important to the event. I remembered my soul-searching in the car and the gray area between reality and fantasy and from such thoughts garnered fresh resolve.

The ceremonies began at last and attention shifted rightfully to the dais. I breathed a sigh of relief.

We were called to attention and the air force band began to play the national anthem.

As the music swelled I relaxed and looked around me. We were on the grounds of the National Aeronautics and Space Administration at Palmdale, California. To my right were several of my Star Trek associates past and future: Nichelle Nichols, otherwise known as Communications Officer Uhura, Gene Roddenberry, the creator of Star Trek and producer of the movie to come, Leonard Nimoy, the inimitable Mr. Spock, George Takei, Mr. Sulu to one and all, Jimmy Doohan, the alterego of Chief Engineer Montgomery "Scotty" Scott, and De Forest Kelley. The occasion was the roll-out of Shuttle Orbiter 101. The day marked the opening of a new era in space transportation. Within a few short years the Shuttle carrier would be hauling space payloads such as sensing satellites and Spacelabs in and out of Earth orbit on a regular basis.

The music subsided and we resumed our seats. Mr. John F. Yardley, the associate administrator, Office of Space Flight, NASA, called for the roll-out to begin. The order was passed through the ranks. The taxiing vehicle appeared around the corner of a building. In tow was Orbiter 101. It began its approach. I noticed in passing that the air force band leader had raised his baton. The carrier was closer now and then closer still. Then it happened. The band leader moved his hands with an emphatic gesture and suddenly we were standing and shaking hands and embracing each other. *The space craft was approaching to the theme music from* "Star Trek." The same chill ran down all our spines. I can't remember seeing a group of people so moved as those in the row beside me. I felt myself close to tears and wasn't the least embarrassed by it. Orbiter 101 was now directly in front of us. Who says there has to be a line between reality and fantasy? Maybe Ronald Colman wasn't crazy, after all. Across the nose of the ship was the word *"ENTERPRISE."*

Star Trek lives! Damn right!

In the nearly ten years since we stopped shooting the television series, the roll-out of Shuttle Orbiter 101 remains my keenest Star Trek-aligned memory.

There have been others, however: fifty science-fiction conventions across the United States and Canada; an appearance on the "Tomorrow" show with De Forest Kelley, Jimmy, and Harlan Ellison; authorship of an animated "Star Trek" episode, denounced as a "commie" by an Idaho potato farmer; guest-starring as a German immigrant in a television show because the "star" they really wanted to play the German immigrant had also once played a Russian and wasn't available (don't ask); discovering new friends in thirty different states; being offered the part of Chekov's *father* by Gene in an earlier proposed version of the film; ongoing letters from troubled teen-agers and happy teen-agers the world over; and the late-night phone call with the promise of "big money" and the "break of a lifetime" for my consent to "star" in a pornographic parody of the series.

Who knows what the ten years following the movie will bring? I don't. I could never have predicted the events of the preceding decade, and I won't even begin to guess what the future holds in store.

What I do know about is mind-trekking on a starship, going around the universe in eighty days, what it was like working on *Star Trek—The Motion Picture* motion picture.

It all started on a hot summer day. . . .

August

WEDNESDAY, AUGUST 2

Today we screen-test for costume and makeup. Does the person fit the makeup? Does the costume fit the person? Does the makeup fit the costume? Will it all fit together? Will everyone have a fit?

10:30 a.m.: I discover Persis Khambatta, who plays Ilia, in the makeup room. I discover her bald head. Not bald, naked. Intriguing, captivating. I want—no—*need* to kiss it. She says, "Of course," the way a mother does to her nine-year-old's timid request for a second cookie. Beautiful women always anticipate aberrant cravings and are, therefore, always gracious in response. Not exactly what I expected—God knows what I expected!—it's bumpy, prickly, a skull with Egyptian #8 base on it. Moral: sometimes it's better to *long* to touch, to be transported by lyric yearnings, than to get makeup on your teeth.

12:11 p.m.: I relate to Leonard Nimoy a conversation I had with a young woman encountered at a Star Trek convention the month before. She, of radiant smile and delightful twinkle, had confessed—twenty seconds after we were introduced—that only with Mr. Spock had she ever achieved sexual completeness. Since she had no interest at all in Mr. Nimoy, these spectacular liaisons occurred, of course, on a different plane. Her priest and two psychiatrists could not persuade her that there was something less than substantial about this relationship, and I succeeded no better than they. She explained that it was only, in fact, because she had seen in the eyes of the omniscient Vulcan a minuscule but, nonetheless, measurable respect for the Russian ensign ("The Apple" "S.T." episode—1967) that she had confided her cherished secret to me at all. Sensing the futility of further discourse, I thereafter remained silent, which, in short order, she construed as accord. A kiss from her fingertips to my cheek and a "ta-ta" over her shoulder as she skipped off were by way of parting. I watched her go suspecting that the "ta-ta" translates in the mother tongue as: "I've always been dependent on the kindness of strangers."

Leonard has little to say after I finish the story. Not so curious, perhaps, for Mr. Spock, but surprising, I feel, for Leonard Nimoy, the social commentator, the astute observer of the human condition. Not so surprising on second thought. I am remembering the letters he used to receive when we were doing the series. What is one man's unique experience is another's everyday mail.

1:30 p.m.: The word has just come down that some of us look too shaggy. Haircuts are in order. The bottom drops out of my stomach. Haircuts have always terrified me. There was a time at Grinnell College in Iowa when I defied the United States Government by refusing to get a "regulation" haircut for the compulsory R.O.T.C. course I was attending. The result was ten trillion demerits, which I would still be working off if I hadn't transferred to U.C.L.A. the following semester.

We still haven't started the screen tests, and so

George and I are instructed to proceed forthwith to the studio barber shop.

Victor, the hair stylist, is terrific. He cleverly tucks the offending locks behind my ears while doing a minimum of snipping. "No one will ever know," he winks. I look at myself in the mirror. Praise be to God, I can still topple temples.

3:00 p.m.: We are now screen-testing makeup and costumes. Turn left—turn right—walk away from camera —walk toward camera. George says we look like beauty pageant contestants. Somebody starts whistling "A Pretty Girl Is Like a Melody," but no one camps; no one even smiles. This is deadly serious stuff, or is it just that we are all feeling too new at this, too unsure that this is really happening after all these years, too concerned that if we break into smiles we'll shatter the reality of this motion picture project and be sent back (like to the penitentiary) to a reality where the phone does not ring and we wait and wait and wait for a *Star Trek* film that never happens?

It's my turn now before the "magic eye." Suddenly everything stops. Major conference: cinematographer, director, costume designer, makeup master hunched and huddling with their backs to me six feet away. Buzz— buzz—buzz. I'm that nine-year-old again and cookies will not fortify me against the exclusion of my peers.

The conclave concludes. Fred Phillips, the artist in charge of creating beauty that is skin deep, approaches solemnly. There's no room for me on their stickball team! I can see it in his eyes. Worse!

"Walter, we're going to have to cut the gray hairs on your chest; they look like hell."

So there it is, folks, the only pre-adolescent with the body foliage of an octogenarian.

The offending follicles are exorcised and I change

from Reuben shirt (a nifty number that fits so tightly my belly button is outlined) to Dress Uniform to Work Outfit (jumpsuit) to Sickbay apparel (I'm supposed to get burned in the story).

There is considerable grumbling from the actors about how the costumes fit and feel. I suspect it has more to do with their "newness," the fact that they are different from what we had worn during the series, than the quality of comfort.

Since there is so much riding on the success of this film, anything different is bound to be a trifle disquieting: Are we rocking the boat? Will the fans be upset by the changes? Familiarity breedeth content. Actually, I think the new designs are terrific. Robert Fletcher, the designer responsible, has succeeded on the three major counts: they are esthetically pleasing, functional, and project well as a future evolvement from current military styles. My wife, Judy, as well as being an actress, is a costume designer. She agrees with me. As far as I'm concerned, that's the final word.

4:25 p.m.: There has been one dominating thread in our conversation throughout the day: the spooky aspect of us all being together again doing Star Trek again after so many years. *"Déjà vu, déjà vu, déjà vu."* The expression may forever replace "They haven't written my character right" as the major refrain of our off-camera palaver. It sounds forced, though—like an actor pushing an emotion he doesn't really feel.

Bill Shatner, our redoubtable Captain James T. Kirk, and Jimmy are off shooting on other projects, but Leonard, De Forest, Nichelle, George, Majel Barrett (Dr. Christine Chapel) and Grace Lee Whitney (Transporter Chief Janice Rand) are all of us here and yet, where is that sense of camaraderie, that feeling of swept away euphoria? It would seem to be in short supply.

I don't know; maybe it's *just* the new uniforms, maybe it's *just* because we have been assembled on a barren soundstage and not on the bridge set; but so far, I sense from everyone that it is not the same as it was. This may be Star Trek, but it isn't the *old* Star Trek. The jury may still side in favor of Thomas Wolfe.

We're through with the tests. George and I trudge toward our dressing rooms having vowed to have a good time on the film. It's a storybook adventure, we tell each other. Who knows what directions our lives will take as the result of our involvement? The thought is indeed titillating. My imagination soars: after *Star Trek* only the best scripts, the juiciest roles. Stardom at last!

Checking out at the front gate, the guard has trouble finding my name on the cast list.

8:00 p.m.: The script we have had until now is the two-hour TV-movie version. We all knew it was going to be rewritten because, among other things, it did not include the character of Spock. A special messenger now delivers the first act and two-thirds of the revised screenplay. I read it slowly, forcing myself not to look ahead for Chekov's speeches. Smart move. The Russian's part is a bit of a disappointment, and canvassing it first would probably have distorted my perception of the story's merit.

Actually, the script looks good to me and, more important, promises to be spectacular film viewing. If the special effects translate to the screen as they are described on the printed page, we will have, quite simply, a winner. Also, there appears to be a scientific discipline in the approach to the writing that is admirable. Our science-oriented fiction fans will rejoice for the input of Jesco von Puttkamer, our technical advisor from NASA. Not to mention fans of adventure, romance, and philosophical statements. The first act and two-thirds seems to have it all, plus a sound story structure. Then why do I go to bed depressed? Mainly because while it is true there are small actors, it is also true there are small parts.

THURSDAY, AUGUST 3

We are still five days away from our production start date, but there is another studio call today. This time it is for publicity stills.

11:30 a.m.: I enter the movie lot resolved to be cool and distant. Write me a small role, will they? Well, I'll show them!

Nobody seems particularly impressed by my evil mood. In fact, it goes unnoticed. Worse, I can't maintain it. Gene comes by looking like an Old English sheepdog. (Overnight I've become obsessed with the length of people's hair.) He has a big hello for each of us and my cockles thaw in spite of myself. I've always been a sucker for a pretty smile.

I see Robert Wise, the director of our movie, again. As always, he is subdued. I can't tell whether he is tired, unhappy, or just preoccupied. He is not an aloof man, but just what kind of man is he? I do not yet know. Maybe it's the huge film successes he has had, or maybe it's the enigmatic character of his character, but I certainly do not feel comfortable in his presence. On the other hand, I don't feel too comfortable in the presence of the guy who brings the morning coffee, either.

I am becoming increasingly more aware of how young everybody is: Linda DeScenna, the set decorator;

Mike Minor and Rick Sternbach, illustrators; Dan Maltese, a set designer; Lee Cole, graphics; Doug Wise, second assistant director; and Kevin Cremin, assistant director trainee. They all appear to be in their twenties or early thirties. I feel positively venerable until I learn that their backgrounds and experience need no apology. Rick, for example, is fresh from NASA, and Lee designed some of the consoles on the B-1 bomber. She is also credited with discovering, before it was too late, that the switches for the toilet flush and the seat ejection on the huge plane had been placed within a fingertip's thickness from each other. Think of the possibilities. "Potty training with a vengeance" is one of a host of images that comes to mind.

Among other things that she and Rick are responsible for is Chekov's weaponry station. We have now convened on the bridge for the photo session, and while waiting for the publicity department to set up, I amble over to my console. My viewer screen hasn't been installed yet, but Lee and Rick assure me that through the magic of rear projection it will eventually record exploding asteroids and space wormholes (whatever those are) in addition to other manner of extraterrestrial phenomena.

I look down at the complicated system of lights and levers and, for the first time, I'm really getting excited; all that brain power, all that man power, all that money that went into constructing this extraordinary-looking equipment—and *I* get to push the buttons! This is even better than 1946, when I was Flash Gordon every day for six months. Time is elastic. If you play your rubber band right, you never have to put away "childish things."

1:25 p.m.: I've finally gotten a fix on what it is the women, at least, object to about the new uniforms.

They do not feel that the unisex look (no bare legs) serves best to underscore their feminine appeal. While it is true that a shapely limb is a joy to behold, the form-fitting uniforms make the prospect of beholding (not to mention holding) other areas of the anatomy equally joyful. It can be unequivocally stated that the women in our company, each and every one, have superior posteriors. What they clearly lack, in their discontent, is a little hindsight.

2:00 p.m.: Bonnie Prendergast, the script person, hands me a manila envelope with the cautionary remark: "It has been cleared by the F.B.I."

Inside are two sheets of paper. One has the blueprint of the weaponry console, and the other a diagram indicating what levers make what systems "operational." There is, as well, an accompanying admonition regarding the reproduction of these sheets, the inference being that the contents are secret, and to view them otherwise is to be in violation of federal law!

Am I about to play a fictional character in a fictional story, or a real officer about to embark on a real secret mission aboard a real spaceship? The more an actor lives his role, the fainter the line between fantasy and reality. I'm beginning to suspect that someone is trying to rub it out altogether. I have been known in the past to respond facetiously to questions concerning the various colored buttons I pushed at my station on the tv series: the blue when I was depressed, the red when I was angry, the purple when I was in a rage, the green when I was feeling envious. Not anymore. I am feeling properly awed and respectful. In fact, I am wondering how much damage the ship will sustain when we crash through the roof of the soundstage on our ascent to the stars.

3:11 p.m.: I've just had approximately 150 publicity shots taken of me at my weaponry console. The next session in about half an hour will be the group photos.

I am preparing to relax (some people can relax; I must prepare to relax) when a complement of executives enters somberly. People who enter places somberly always portend disasters. The happier the place, the more merriment and expectation that abound, the worse their portending. A cold chill runs up my spine. Even paranoids have enemies, however, and I am dead right. The worst possible news. They've looked at the screen tests from yesterday, and George and I each need another haircut.

Victor again practices his special form of legerdemain. Despite the lopping of additional tresses, I will not yet be mistaken for Dumbo.

3:54 p.m.: Back on the set. We're all gathered on the bridge now, around the conn for the group shots. While we wait for the "Rinky-Dinks," "Baby Juniors," and "K-Tens" (lights) to be positioned, Bill illustrates dramatically the myriad problems he foresees in climbing in and out of his command seat. Everyone quietly stands and watches as Bill takes center stage and pleads his case: animated gestures, irresistible eye contact, moving oratory. In all, very theatrical, very convincing. Those who must contend with the changes he seeks nod hypnotically. We all nod hypnotically. We're all his audience.

There are reasons why some actors are leading men, get the girl and captain starships—even ten years later —while others eternally push buttons. For the first time that eerie feeling of familiarity for times bygone begins to creep up my neck. Despite myself, the words escape my lips: "My God, nothing has changed!" De Forest is standing nearby. Our looks hold for a moment. I can't be sure he is sharing my experience. I would like to believe he is. It's lonely being the only one who understands such profound concepts.

5:30 p.m.: I've just finished with another costume fitting and am on my way home. I've only been at the studio for six hours, but I feel exhausted. I feel like I've been on the film for months. It would seem that in recreating my role I am also recreating the circumstances surrounding it. In our series days I was always drained after a long day at Paramount, and now, back at Paramount, back on the bridge, back as Chekov, I'm back being tired. Somebody should do a treatise on the psycho-neurotic nature of fatigue. Oh, well, nothing scheduled for Friday. I have all day tomorrow to rest up from my memories.

FRIDAY, AUGUST 4

9:00 a.m.: The phone rings. It's Doug, the second assistant director. "Could you get here by eleven, Walter? Mr. Roddenberry and Mr. Wise would like to talk to you about getting another haircut."

MONDAY, AUGUST 7

"Look, up in the sky! It's a bird! It's a plane! It's . . . the Enterprise!!" *No lie. Today, nine and one-half years after we filmed our last episode of the "Star Trek" television series, we are refueling. There's an alien force up there threatening to destroy our Earth. We've got to get going. "Rolling, camera, action!"*

5:55 a.m.: Good morning, Universe.

7:30 a.m.: Arrive at studio and raring to go.

7:45 a.m.: Through makeup and raring to go.

8:00 a.m.: Into my costume—dress uniform—and raring to go.

11:10 a.m.: "My "rare" is getting a little well done. The first shot is very tricky and we're still trying to properly coordinate all its component parts. The setup involves a 300-degree sweep of the bridge, catching on cue important physical action and specific lines of dialogue between various ship personnel. The timing has to be perfect and is made all the more difficult to attain because of the presence of several new crew members who also have action and dialogue and must be included in the pan.

The six new actors who will be with us for as long as we will be shooting on the bridge are: Iva Lane, Momo Yashima, Ralph Brannen (Momo's husband), Franklyn Seales, Ralph Byers, and Billy Van Zandt, who plays the only bridge alien.

In the shot we are all overlapping each other's speeches as we work at our posts checking the functions of the refitted *Enterprise* prior to lift-off after two and one-half years of dry dock. We rehearse it several times more and are then excused from the set while lights are repositioned.

While waiting, new pages are delivered to each of the actors. I blanche visibly (I am told) when I discover that Chekov has a mouthful of incomprehensible technical jargon which he must make his own in the next ten minutes. Good Heavens! It's only the first three hours and already I feel my throat constricting, my stomach convexing, my brain convulsing.

"Phaser targeting monitor, phaser torpedoes operational . . ." I repeat them over and over again like a prayer . . . Hail Mary full of grace. . . . Photon torpedoes operational . . .

12:15 p.m.: Reprieve! Lunch break. I will have at least an hour to get the lines right before being called upon to do them on film.

I look down at my uniform. Whoops! Wrong military braid on my sleeve. Sub-lieutenant instead of full lieutenant. In the old days, before I understood the dedication to detail that is a characteristic of Star Trek fans everywhere, I would probably have ignored the error in rank. After all, who would notice? About thirty million Trekkies, that's who.

I am told to change into my General Work uniform. If the braid isn't corrected in time, we will shoot the scene in that outfit.

I go to lunch. Find a marble in the street. On the spot I decide that it will be my talisman. I shall carry it with me always and with it I will give *Star Trek* the best performance of my life. Don't ask.

12:50 p.m.: Back from lunch. Braid corrected. Out of General Work costume and back into Dress uniform. I'm beginning to feel like Gypsy Rose Lee!

1:44 p.m.: We're still trying to get the first shot of the day. A principal problem is the anti-gravitational "ladder" on which one of the crew members, working above the bridge deck, is supposed to float up and out of the shot as the camera pans past him. The ladder is a disc on which he stands, and he and it are attached by very thin wires (not visible on film) to an overhanging pulley mechanism. The wires are connected to loops on either side of his specially built belt, and the difficulty seems to be in getting them to pull evenly.

John McKnight, the extra who plays the crew member, keeps tipping as he is hauled up, with the result that he appears about to slip off the ladder. This piece of business is, of course, only one small part of the hugely complicated setup that includes all the actors talking at once and the camera moving steadily past them, singling each one out at the appropriate moment. Needless to say, on the rare occasions that John doesn't tip, something else goes wrong.

Everyone is very anxious to get that first shot in the can, to get this picture officially underway, and the frustration is beginning to manifest itself in sharp under-the-breath expletives. Through it all, Director Wise remains imperturbable. He even smiles occasionally. I don't know him any better than before, but I'm beginning to like him more. In the face of difficulty he remains quite human. Not so casual a virtue as it sounds. I've seen plenty of Mr. Hydes in this business who had been Dr. Jekylls until the test tubes began to effervesce.

3:00 p.m.: Hurrah! The first *Star Trek* shot of the day, of the year, of the decade is in the can. We now set up for the second shot: James Kirk making his appearance on the bridge for the first time after again being given command of the *Enterprise*.

The initial rehearsal commences. The Captain steps out of the elevator, and Sulu, Uhura, and Chekov rush to greet him. . . . And there it is, folks, instant euphoria. In this first run-through, anyway, I'm not acting. My elation at seeing the Captain again isn't pretend stuff— because it isn't just the good feeling of the *Enterprise* crew being back together again; it's also the extraordinary sensation of working again with all these people I haven't traded dialogue with in nine and one-half years. *This* is *déjà vu*, that one eerie, joyful, special focused moment of familiarity. At this instant I feel like kissing Bill and Nichelle and George. The world is beautiful, life is golden, love abounds. I am engulfed with a sense of the romantic. I could walk on air (without support wires). And here I thought I was a die-hard cynic with a cranky disposition.

Several takes later I am wondering if I'll *ever* get a closeup in this fifteen-million-dollar opus.

Between takes there is considerable talk about how long we will be working on the picture. The contract guarantee for most of us is five weeks, but if the first day is any indication, the bridge scenes alone may take that long. During the long periods of waiting we buoy ourselves with speculation about added plunder and bloated coffers.

6:17 p.m.: We finally "pull the plug." Shooting is completed for the day. I trudge (my standard gait at the close of each day) to my dressing room. I remove the company athletic supporter (no underwear lines in the costumes, please) and change into my clothes. The guard at the gate recognizes me and waves as I leave, but it doesn't lift my weary spirits. For one thing, after so long an absence before the camera, my first day back again as Chekov is not Hamlet's soliloquy. For another, I've lost my goddamn marble!

7:11 p.m.: There is a large exotic plant on my dining room table. It is from Michael Eisner, president and chief operating officer of Paramount Pictures. I am wondering if maybe I could have a lucky plant instead of a lucky marble.

TUESDAY, AUGUST 8

Second day of shooting, second day preparing for lift-off. We got half a page of story in the can yesterday. In both the figurative and literal sense, we have no way to go but up.

5:00 a.m.: I've set the alarm for 6:15 but my head won't cooperate. I stumble toward the bathroom in the dark. First order of business: check the mirror and see what havoc the lost sleep hath wrought. Gadzooks! My face looks like the last bastion against a monstrous tidal wave—not just bags, sandbags! My wife, Judy, hears me groan. In an action beyond the call of duty, she leaves the warmth of bed and volunteers to help.

She is back from the kitchen shortly and applying sliced cucumber to my epidermal puffs. It is an astringent, she says, and insists it will tighten the skin. I am too tired to resist. I am reminded of all those stories I've heard about fading movie stars and their excesses in pursuit of the illusion of youth. Observing myself now with green rinds and little seeds plastered to my skin, I resolve hereafter to be more tolerant of other people's neuroses.

6:45 a.m.: Judy is reading the *Los Angeles Times* as I depart. She calls after me that my horoscope says to be "enterprising" today.

8:00 a.m.: I am handed a new page of dialogue on the set. It is a checklist that Chekov must check off (I've waited ten years to say that) as the ship leaves dry dock. The other actors receive similar sheets. Mine is as follows:

CHEKOV	COMPUTER VOICE
Targeting Scanners	Check
Intruder Alert Scanners	Functioning
Phaser Power Accumulators	Standby
Phaser Manual Overrides	Automatic mode
Phaser Targeting	Standby
Photon Torpedo Load Status	Full
Photon Torpedo Targeting	Standby
Photon Torpedo Manual Overrides ..	Automatic mode
All Deflector Screen Power Levels ..	Optimum
Deflector Screen Placements	Automatic mode
Forcefield Power Levels	Optimum

11:18 a.m.: Naturally, I get it right in every rehearsal up until we actually start shooting the scene. Then, forget it—at least I did. Again and again and again. The fault, dear Brutus, lies not in the stars, but in that mother——— marble. I think I'll coin a famous saying: "When there is a hole in your memory, look for a hole in your pocket."

11:42 a.m.: It turns out that it doesn't much matter whether I know the lines or not. Ditto for the other actors who have been handed tongue-twisting technical dialogue this morning. This piece of business (checking the functioning of our respective stations) is just another setup from the scene begun yesterday when we were all talking at once, and it is now decided to shoot the action in a master shot and record all the simultaneous dialogue separately off camera. The positioning of the camera and the lens being employed are such that facial detail will not be discernible in this sequence. Consequently, it will not be necessary to synchronize lip movement with sound. I get to do the lines again, this time with the script in my hand. I'm fantastic! Oh, for the good old days of radio.

1:00 p.m.: I've had my lunch break and now go directly to the makeup room on Stage Ten. (We always have our makeup redone after lunch.) The bridge set, the engineering set, the ship's corridors, officers' quarters, transporter, and sickbay are all across the alley on Stage Nine and are, therefore, very convenient to the makeup room. Persis is in the chair as I enter, preparing to have her dome shaved again. I am startled to see that her hair has already grown back a half an inch. She offers to let me stroke her head. How can I refuse? This time it is soft and fluffy, not prickly. I'm beginning to feel like Lenny in *Of Mice and Men*.

"Tell me about the rabbits, George."

Speaking of George: people keep calling me George, not Walter. George thinks it's hilarious. Particularly since no one calls him Walter.

Susan Sackett, Gene Roddenberry's executive assistant, Rosanna Attias and Michelle Billy, secretaries over at the *Star Trek* offices, have been stopping by these last few days full of enthusiasm for the project. They have seen this production take shape over many months (in Susan's case, years) and have lived and died with the announced start dates and subsequent postponements that have had our launch lurching. They are quick to say how good all the actors look and how wonderful they believe the film will be. In these early days when we are all feeling our way, wondering to ourselves whether we can indeed pull off *Star Trek—The Motion Picture,* it is reassuring to have these young women rallying to the cause. Thank you Susan, Rosanna, and Michelle.

5:20 p.m.: I've not been on camera all afternoon, but when Gene bounces ebulliently onto the set full of kind words to the cast for yesterday's dailies (the filmed sequences that were printed from Monday's shooting), I feel buoyed, as well. We're going to have a hit! WE'RE GOING TO HAVE A HIT!! What a wonderful thing it is to know that divine Providence is looking out especially for us!

5:52 p.m.: The whipped cream on my cheery pie of life is the personalized sterling-silver Tiffany key ring left for each of us in our dressing rooms at the close of the day by Jeff Katzenberg, vice-president in charge of motion pictures for Paramount Pictures Corp. A nice gesture. It seems we're inundated with nice gestures. With such good feelings all around, how can we help but have a hit? And to think we already have two whole days of shooting in the can!

WEDNESDAY, AUGUST 9

Today Kirk speaks to his devoted crew and tells Commander Willard Decker, played by Stephen Collins, he is taking over the Enterprise. *Ilia makes her first entrance aboard the ship.*

7:25 a.m.: At the studio. My call is 7:45, but I keep waking up earlier and earlier.

A telltale sign that this production is coming apart, that morale is weakening, that pride and self-respect are crumbling: someone has forgotten to include a jockstrap with my uniform this morning.

I overhear Doug, the second assistant, talking on the phone about kids and midgets exactly three feet, four feet, and five feet tall to be used in engineering. The engine room is a marvelous set that has been designed with a forced perspective. The set pieces in the foreground are largest and diminish proportionately in size as they recede toward the back. Also, the design lines dovetail, forming the wide open end of a "V" in front, gradually closing toward a point at the rear. The purpose, of course, is to give the twenty-foot-long room the illusion of great depth.

The structure works beautifully even just *standing* in front of it. On camera, with a painted background at the base of the narrow end continuing the perspective two-dimensionally, the sense of distance will be extraordinary. Now, I'm told, that to underscore the effect they are going to place three small people, exactly five feet, four feet, and three feet tall—from foreground to background—along the twenty-foot-long set. Their positioning will force the eye to further accept the illusion of depth while denying the difference in their heights. Damn clever, these natives.

My son, Josh, just happens to be four feet, one-half inch on the button. I know he'd love to be in the movie. I mention it to Doug. He says he'll "get back to me." There are no words in the film business that are surer death than those.

8:45 a.m.: Among other things we have been shooting these past three days is the bridge sequence that introduces Sulu, Uhura, and Chekov into the story. I have been grappling with the idea of mentioning to Mr. Wise that there have been no closeups or even medium shots of Chekov scheduled here. After all, this *is* the first time he is seen—his "entrance," so to speak.

Kirk has an entrance (at the top of the story), Spock and McCoy have distinct entrances (onto the ship), Uhura and Sulu have been recorded in tight single shots as they are first seen, but Chekov has not been so favored. Each of the Star Trek regulars has his/her coterie of fans out there who would revel in the opportunity to cheer his/her favorite's first appearance in a Star Trek uniform after so long. I would hope that Pavel Chekov is not excepted from that group.

Shouldn't this omission be brought to the director's attention? Perhaps he isn't familiar with the fan following the supporting players enjoy.

We are setting up for another group shot. I decide not to mull the pros and cons any further. Impetuously, I make my feelings known to Mr. Wise. What a mistake. What an incredible mistake! He speaks softly, even gently, but nonetheless, unequivocally.

"Don't worry about camera angles," he admonishes. "Please don't make those actorish suggestions again."

I am thoroughly put down. All the more because from his point of view he is dead right. Performance, not camera angles, should be my concern. My God, just think what he would say if he saw me with cucumber slices all over my pan! I may never recover from my humiliation. It comes at me in shock waves, setting my face to twitching, my body to shuddering like those poor unfortunates who walk the New York streets babbling tormentedly to themselves. Guilt, always bobbing just below the surface, now rears its ugly countenance. If only I had some dry olive switches with which to properly atone.

What makes the situation even more depressing is the knowledge that, right or wrong, I am totally committed to the principle of the "squeaky wheel." If only I could learn to keep my mouth shut. Distressed as I am, I know I am doomed to commit the same sin again and again whenever I am convinced that my rights, real or imagined, need defending. Talk about your Sisyphus!

There is some speculation on the set regarding Steve Collins, cast to play Captain Decker. Steve is tall, blond, and blue-eyed—definitely your leading-man type, and, in fact, his character does have a romantic interest in our story. Why, we are wondering, is there a Captain Decker when there is also a Captain Kirk? Does Bill have an "out" clause regarding *Star Trek* sequels? Is Steve being groomed to take his place if there is a second feature or a return to a television series? Rumors run rampant. I approach our newest crew member and ask him directly if there is anything in his contractual agreement regarding the continuation of his services beyond this project. He says no. I have no reason to disbelieve him. At this point, at least, we can all stop wondering.

12:12 p.m.: Just before we break for lunch, Robert Wise says that he wants to pick up a closeup of Chekov after lunch. Ostensibly, it is said to Danny McCauley, the first assistant director, but the words are spoken loud enough to be heard ten feet away. I am standing nine feet away. Apparently Mr. Wise has also seen those poor tortured souls on the pavement of the Big Apple. He doesn't want to add to their number. I am overwhelmed by the sensitivity of his loudness. Thank you, Mr. Wise, you are truly a gentle-man.

2:00 p.m.: The first successful gate-crasher. A young man named Steve had been hanging around outside the studio for two days. He had hocked everything he owned to come out west from New York for the express purpose of getting on the *Star Trek* set.

Steve got lucky when he overheard an invited guest of George's, a man who works to pass transit legislation in Washington, introduce himself to the security man at the gate. He then waited until a changing of the guards and, using the previous fellow's identity, managed to get a clearance onto the lot. Not at all bashful, he sought George out and gleefully recounted the story to him. Moral: with perseverance, almost anything is possible—even passing for a tall black government lobbyist when you're a small Caucasian college student.

2:33 p.m.: My first closeup in the movie—not the introductory sequence, but one where I see Ilia for the first time. It's just a reaction shot, but already I'm not satisfied. I let some time go by and then ask the director his policy regarding actors attending dailies. He says they are welcome. I'm not sure I am relieved or disappointed.

4:35 p.m.: Gene comes by again. He's even more animated than he was yesterday. He loves Tuesday's dailies.

"It's bigger, it's brighter, but it's definitely *Star Trek!*"

I am happy for Gene on many counts, not the least of which is his twofold loyalty to the *Star Trek* actors and the characters they play. It was he who time and again insisted that *all* the series regulars be included in the plans for a new *Star Trek* vehicle, and it was he, almost totally alone, who fought to maintain the character integrity of each member of the *Enterprise* crew. If there is a lack of definition in personality and relationship for some of the bridge officers in the current script version, the failing is not Gene Roddenberry's. I know how hard he tried.

5:52 p.m.: We're already almost a full day behind our shooting schedule, but it's getting late and Robert Wise will not work into the evening hours. He is meticulous in his approach to shooting a film and feels that if he goes beyond twelve hours on the set, he will begin to lose his edge. I think I began to lose mine around 11:00 this morning.

Thursday was supposed to be a day off for the bridge personnel, but we are now handed "call sheets" for tomorrow with the scenes we didn't get to today. We'll be back.

As I head for home I am thinking about the studio theater where today's footage will be screened at noon tomorrow. It will be the first time I'll see myself again as Chekov after almost ten years. It is a consideration that points up one of the most unique and ironic aspects of the Star Trek phenomenon. After so many years the Star Trek following remains militant, vociferous, amatory. But is it fixated in 1966–1969?

Over and over and over again the seventy-nine episodes of the series have been shown in syndication, and not one time in one episode during all the intervening years has an actor's jowls hung more heavily, has his pate reflected light more brightly, has his features coarsened, his facial lines deepened. The genius of the makeup department notwithstanding, in August of 1978 we are different, we have changed. It's only natural. Or is it? Why do I feel that I must protest, that I must apologize for the inevitable?

The cover article in an *Esquire* Magazine issue a couple of years back said that television viewers have a passionate allegiance to the stars of popular series but reject them summarily when they attempt playing other characters in other vehicles. It is disconcerting enough to find yourself in competition with other characters you have played, but, at least, if the character is written well and the story is interesting, you have a fighting chance. It's damn near debilitating, however, to discover yourself—in a youth-oriented, youth-revering society—in a competition you cannot win, a competition against your younger self. Hey, *I* believe that with "maturity" comes character and depth and all the other qualities that make people more interesting; I just can't speak for the people who change channels and buy tickets.

Tomorrow I'll get an idea as to how great a toll ten years has taken. Of course, if I were *less* "mature," I might consider the alternative of ramming a four-ton semi on the way home, landing in a hospital for several months and avoiding tomorrow altogether.

THURSDAY, AUGUST 10

Today we begin the scene where the Enterprise *lifts off after two and one-half-years in dry dock and nine and one-half years in syndication.*

5:45 a.m.: As my head was shutting down in sleep last night, I heard out of the corner of my ear that the New York Yankees were losing 7 to 3 to Milwaukee going into the bottom of the ninth. Now, when I turn on the radio this morning, I am pleasantly surprised to learn that the Yanks scored five runs in their last turn at bat and won. The change of score is significant to me beyond my rooting interest in the New York team. I am made acutely aware that there is a world "out there" and that the more occupied and preoccupied I am and will be with Star Trek, the less real and operational that world will become. That knowledge is both, at the same time, disturbing and reassuring. I am frequently overwhelmed by how short life is, and the prospect of it slipping past me unnoticed while I labor cloistered on a movie soundstage is, indeed, disquieting. On the other hand, there is the comfort of knowing that I can always escape back into the real world if events transpire too traumatically for me in this insulated environment (in other words, if they don't give Chekov more lines to say).

8:05 a.m.: Then, again, sometimes you can have your slice of life and eat it, too. While Fred Phillips applies panstick and eyeliner, Steve Collins, in the next chair to mine, admits to being a Yankee fan also. Here is my connection to the outside world. For several minutes we revel in the last-gap heroics of the Bronx Bombers, oblivious to the ministrations of our respective makeup artists.

9:35 a.m.: Dick Keenan, a professor from Maryland, is doing a book on Robert Wise. We talk briefly about the director. I recount my exchange with him of the day before. He finds it interesting because he is looking for more detail on the man's relationship with his actors. In passing, he tells a story about Robert Wise with Spencer Tracy and James Cagney when he worked with them. I'm a cynic and, therefore, force the feeling of awe that hurdles my bunions from rising farther. All the same, Spencer Tracy and James Cagney, Jeez!

12:00 p.m.: The dailies. A misnomer; the deathlies. I envision slipping into the studio theater unnoticed and sitting anonymously in a deep chair at the back of the room. Egads, I'm the first to arrive! I am joined and flanked by Susan and Michelle from the *Star Trek* offices.

Two views of me flicker across the screen. The first is a three-shot that is okay. The second is the very tight closeup smile reaction to Ilia's entrance onto the bridge. I don't look like the dead dog I once saw floating in the Hudson River engorged and bug-eyed, but beyond that I won't commit myself. Gene, laughing, calls out in the dark, "That kid has a nice smile."

After all these years I still don't know how I come across on the screen. For the sake of mental health I decide to put my faith in the Roddenberry remark.

2:15 p.m.: The scene we are preparing now is the send-off of the good ship *Enterprise* after two and one-half years of refitting and overhauling. The director calls George, Nichelle, Bill, Steve, and me together for a reading of the pages across the alley on Stage Ten.

Two tables are placed end to end, with Mr. Wise at the head. The rest of us, like so many perfectly pro-grammed automatons, unconsciously choose the chairs whose distance from the director most accurately re-flects our billing in the credits. Bill and Steve sit closest. The others, in appropriate order, sit farther away. There is certainly no written law regarding these juxtaposi-tions. On the other hand, the movie business is full of unwritten laws.

I have no lines in the sequence we are rehearsing, but I am, nonetheless, acting like mad: eyes misty with elation, lips tightly set against too much emotion, nos-trils moderately flared in determination. What a per-formance!

After several run-throughs, a couple of anecdotes are related. I mention seeing *Touch of Evil* on the tube the night before and Robert Wise talks about Orson Welles. We discover that he was the editor on both *Citizen Kane* and *The Magnificent Ambersons*.

"When the man was fully concentrated on one project as he was with *Kane*," says our mentor, "he came as close to genius as the history of film has ever known."

I have always accepted Welles's brilliance in a sort of detached, impersonal way. Hereafter, when Orson Welles's name is mentioned, I will beam with pride. I mean, his editor forty years ago is my director now. We're practically related!

3:00 p.m., 4:00 p.m., 5:00 p.m.: The afternoon drags on. I have been in makeup and costume since 8:45 this morning and still have not worked. The scene we rehearsed earlier is being shot now, but since I have no lines my dewy eyes and thin lips remain a neglected resource. There is something else to consider, too: my new station on the bridge is in a pocket or alcove beyond the circumferential line of the bridge. It occurs to me that in most master shots (the angles encompassing the greatest amount of bridge area) I will not be seen and consequently not called upon. To be sure, I want to be seen in this movie, but equally important, I want to participate, to be a part of this project.

I am becoming depressed—worse, morose. I envision my life ahead on this show as an indistinguishable run of days in which I am waiting on the front step, waiting in the parlor, waiting in the wings for a call that never comes. Something between Kafka and Williams, I decide.

Gene comes by again and Nichelle, unbeknownst to me, approaches him on my behalf: "Walter is on the bridge. Shouldn't he be in the shot?" Gene concurs, she tells me later, but nothing changes. All the same, that was nice of Nichelle. After my first-day exchange with our director, I have decided, squeaky wheel or no, not to again push that subject myself.

Jon Povill, the associate producer, happens over. I am resolved to suffer in silence, to deal with the situation as a professional. But he is too insistent, too compelling. I pour out my troubles. He listens silently, nodding occasionally. I feel worse afterward. If only he hadn't loosened my tongue, forced me to reduce myself to a puerile whine. If only he hadn't said, "Hi, Walter."

6:06 p.m.: Time to go home. They'll be shooting in the transporter room tomorrow and I'm not involved. Grace Lee Whitney, Transporter Chief Janice Rand, is in charge of the transporter room in this script. As long a time away from "S.T." as it has been for us, it has been even longer for her. Tomorrow is her big day. I try to imagine her feelings. The vampire in me emerges. I would like to steal in on her this night, find the right vein, suck up her excitement, that very special excitement that I'm convinced happens only to actors, and experience it for myself.

I would come by tomorrow and root her return personally, but I'll be spending the day getting ready for a flight to Joplin, Missouri, for a Star Trek convention. All the same, welcome back, Grace Lee. Nice to have you aboard.

SATURDAY, AUGUST 12

A new day. Just barely. I climb aboard an American Airlines jet at 1:50 A.M. I'm in Dallas by 4:30. Two-hour lay-over until I start on the next leg of my journey.

6:35 a.m.: At last the Frontier Airlines plane rolls to a stop in front of my gate. I gulp hard. It's a two-engine prop! A *turbo* prop, they tell me. Don't let them fool you. It's got propellers, and if they don't go 'round, the airplane don't stay up. I also learn that en route to Joplin we make stops at Port Smith and Fayetteville. I have been told that ninety percent of all air accidents occur on take-off and landing. Not only am I about to quadruple my chances of not surviving this trip, but I'm now convinced that my remains will be eaten by wild pigs in the swamps of Arkansas.

Between Fayetteville and Joplin, the pilot comes back and hunches beside my aisle seat. He would like an autograph. I try to set aside the image of an empty cockpit and, noticing that other passengers are craning their necks, I assume a posture of dignity and importance. I sign with a flare and smile tolerantly the way a benign overlord should with his vassal.

After he leaves I stand up, giving all a chance to view the entire personage, and move gracefully toward the bathroom at the front of the plane. I swing wide the door and am immediately claustrophobic. It is the size of a cleaved closet. Too late to turn back. All eyes are upon me. I enter. The dual close-and-lock mechanism had apparently not been invented when this plane was built. Inadvertently, I fasten the lock latch without sliding the separate close bolt.

I am firmly ensconced (there is no other way to be in such tight quarters) when we are caught in a succession of air pockets and the bathroom door flies open. I look up and find myself staring into the faces of several passengers poised with pens and autograph paper. Famous saying: "It is difficult to maintain an air of dignity and importance when one's pants lay in disarray about one's ankles."

5:00 p.m.: Joplin is a nice city, but very hot and very humid in August. Also, if a truck hits a light pole at the other end of town, you give your one-hour speech to 500 people in the dark.

MONDAY, AUGUST 14

They're still shooting in the transporter room. I will not be called in again today.

11:45 a.m.: I have a drink at Nickodels with Marguerite Michaels, a writer who is doing an article on *Star Trek* for *Parade Magazine.* Here it is only one week into production, at least a full year before the film is released, and already an issue as formidable as *Parade* is looking to us for a cover story. If this magazine reflects the interest of the national community, we sure as hell had better produce a terrific motion picture. What a responsibility! I decide to order another drink.

2:30 p.m.: I take my kids to the park and we build sand castles. Never once as a child or thereafter did I ever build sand castles. Frankly, I always thought they were a little corny. But I build them now and I do so unself-consciously and joyfully. I mull this over and decide it's easy to be corny in a sandbox when you are in reality a different person entirely: one who talks funny and who, for at least five weeks, will be on a secret starship mission for the Federation.

7:00 p.m.: My 8:45 call for the morning is no longer viable. Doug has called and said that they'll let me know by noon tomorrow whether we'll be back on the bridge at all on Tuesday. They're still in the transporter room.

TUESDAY, AUGUST 15

The sequence they have been shooting in the transporter room concerns a malfunction of the equipment.

Noon: It's a case of life imitating art. The equipment they are using to shoot the malfunctioning transporter equipment is malfunctioning. We won't return to the bridge today.

WEDNESDAY, AUGUST 16

The Enterprise *is still trying to lift off. Considering the "time means money" adage, this may yet be the most traumatic lift-off since Icarus's wings melted.*

9:30 a.m.: I arrive at the studio and am told to remain in civvies until told otherwise.

10:00 a.m., 11:00 a.m., 12:00 p.m.: I spend the time before lunch in my dressing room writing and talking to Nichelle. I knew she had been associated with NASA earlier in the year, but not to the fascinating extent she describes this morning.

Before she started recruiting women and minorities for the space program in a coast-to-coast tour of colleges and conventions (engineering conventions, not S.T.), there were approximately 1,600 NASA applicants. Of these, only sixty were women. There were virtually no blacks in this group. After her "Space" trek, the numbers had changed to 600 women, 1,000 minority-class applicants, and more than 8,000 people overall. I'm very impressed.

She really seems committed. I envy her the opportunity to influence history. Maybe one of the people she motivated to apply for the space program will be the first person on Saturn. Pretty heady stuff. I can see it now: "Dear Mr. Chekov, I'm nine years old and I watch 'Star Trek' all the time. You're my favorite and because of you I won't drink anything but vodka."

1:15 p.m.: I am back from lunch, sitting on the sound-stage and still waiting to be called. Leonard comes over, sees me with pen and paper and says laughingly: "What are you writing, a book about the making of the movie? Ha-ha-ha!"

"Absolutely," I reply. "Ho-ho-ho!"

I haven't told anybody I'm doing this journal, and I really do think it's funny that without realizing it, he hit it right on the nose cone.

1:30 p.m.: The first casualty of our production: we've lost an actor. Actually, it happened last week, but I just learn about it now. She comes from the ranks of the six additional bridge personnel who field the occasional dialogue and business that is not specifically ours. It has been determined that the bridge looks too cluttered and that since Momo, the released actress, is the only one who has not yet been identified with a particular station, she is the logical choice to be discontinued. There is obviously no malice in the decision, nor any personal indictment of the dismissed actor. It could just as easily have been one of the others had it been they and not she to be photographed apart from a console. Furthermore, although it is implicit that these crew members will work with us so long as there are bridge scenes, it is also true that the contracts they signed guaranteed them only one week's work. She had had that.

I am now sitting here wondering why I feel so compelled to defend the actions of the company. I know. It's because I am an actor, too, and I empathize with her, and, because being an actor, being slightly unstable, I would like to believe that when actions are taken that we have no control over, that affect our lives, they are done so as judiciously, as fairly, as possible.

1:45 p.m.: I wander around the soundstage and stop at what now appears to be the completed, fully operational engine block. Fan——tastic! Up until now I've only experienced the esthetic wonder of this forced-perspective set. I had not yet felt its surging life. The engine block, its very heart, was still in construction.

Now it stands before me, an amalgam of extravagant glass shapes rising three stories high. More impressive yet are the internal machinations of the huge structure. Within the body of the engine, light beams are rear-screen projected and bounce off carefully placed reflectors to create the illusion of combusting gases. The lights swirl and dart and appear to be in a state of fission. Different color filters add to the extraordinary effect. Incredible!

2:15 p.m.: Invitations to three different parties are now extended: Persis has invited the cast and brass to an East Indian restaurant next Wednesday night; Rosanna has come by with news of a birthday party for Gene after shooting on Friday; a fan of Star Trek named Richard has invited us to his house for a September 2 gathering. I'll be at the New York Star Trek convention then, but the others should be fun.

It has been discovered that the lens on the 65-mm

camera has not functioned properly, and parts of two days' shooting will have to be redone. This afternoon is being devoted to reshooting the work recorded last Thursday. I didn't work last Thursday. I'm considering taking up jogging as a full-time occupation.

I also learn that there is considerable concern over the special effects promised by the contracted company and not yet delivered. Gad, the plot thickens! What next?!

3:38 p.m.: Marguerite Michaels from *Parade Magazine* has finally received a clearance onto the set. She is the first reporter to do so. It's a tricky situation. Paramount, of course, wants the publicity, but they are worried about interest peaking too early and then dissipating before the picture is released. There is also the danger of someone getting hold of classified data—like what the story is about—and publishing it in advance of the film's premiere.

John Rothwell and his assistant, Suzanne Gordon, the Paramount publicists attached to our show, are the ones who must deal with these myriad ramifications. To his credit, John is almost always smiling. I don't think his job is too easy. He now accompanies Ms. Michaels onto our soundstage. This is a no-nonsense wry young lady (sorry, young *woman*) who has little truck with tinsel and pretense. It is fun watching that cold eye of reality turn wide with wonder as she is led from bridge, to engineering, to transporter, to sickbay, and down the long stretches of winding, shiny corridor. Fantasy is beauty when it hath charms to soothe the most severe critic.

6:00 p.m.: "Good night, Walter. We'll definitely get to you tomorrow." Play a few more bars, Sam; I think I've heard that tune before.

THURSDAY, AUGUST 17

In today's schedule McCoy appears on the bridge for the first time and celestial bodies become strange elongated shapes as the Enterprise, *now sailing along at warp drive, gets caught in a time-matter distortion.*

6:20 a.m.: Happy birthday, Josh. I'm up and out before the day's first tears, blasphemies, and giggles are spent.

7:45 a.m.: Fred Phillips is doing my makeup again this morning. He was the principal craftsman in the shaping of Spock's ears back in our television days, and he is with us again shaping aliens out of latex. In my case, feeling as I do like the undead this morning, he is just trying to create the illusion of life. Fred is our one non-executive link with "Star Trek," the TV series. More important, he is a vital link in the history of film-making itself. He's been in the business fifty years and has a million stories to tell. I keep telling him he should write a book, but he never will because he won't reveal the names of the actors, writers, producers, and directors who populate his marvelously salacious stories. Fred Phillips and his ethical precepts are obviously from another era.

5:30 p.m.: The scenes scheduled for today were: No. 123 (McCoy's entrance onto the bridge), No. 127 (the beginning of the wormhole jeopardy), and Nos. 129 through 134 (as we get sucked deeper into the wormhole and simultaneously discover we are on a collision course with an asteroid).

The latter scenes include my first lines on film since the first day of production: "Photon torpedoes armed" —"Torpedoes away"—"We're out of it"—"Negative damage report, sir"—"No casualties, sir." I have repeated them over and over to myself perhaps a hundred times since 7:45 this morning. Dusk is fast approaching and I have not yet been called upon to immortalize them on celluloid. Call it a wild hunch, but I got this crazy feeling they're not going to get to me again today.

FRIDAY, AUGUST 18

> Tomorrow and tomorrow and tomorrow,
> creeps in this petty pace from day to day.
> —Shakespeare: *Macbeth* V.v.

On the other hand:

> Tomorrow to fresh woods, and pastures new.
> —John Milton: *Lycidas*

I am convinced that today is my day, today I shall be working!

8:00 a.m.: I am through makeup and studying the diagrams of my console so that I can properly load and fire the photon torpedoes.

"How much like Chekov is Koenig?" I've been asked that time and again. Now, I am wondering about it myself; *photon torpedoes, weaponry console*—the words chill the very marrow. I'm not sure Walter Koenig could justify the destruction of one life for the salvation of all mankind, and here is my alter ego at the crisis moment prepared to hit the "red" button. No wonder I have found myself answering with a self-conscious joke questions regarding my new station aboard the *Enterprise*. Somehow I feel I am betraying someone –(my conscience?) with Chekov's always-poised-slightly indented index finger. On the other hand, part of our prime directive is to avoid bloodshed and wage peace. On the other hand, Klingons are people, too. On the other hand (in the celestial environs in which we operate, it is possible to be quadruple-handed), I am an actor, and an actor's responsibility . . . Oh, hell, it's too early to cogitate, to agitate, to remonstrate. *"Damn* the torpedoes, full speed ahead!"

Funny line: I'm still being called George. George continues to think it's hysterical. He asks Susan Sackett if she sees a resemblance. "Only around the eyes," she replies.

I was talking to one of the painters about the durability of Star Trek and it occurred to me that the TV series was like coitus interruptus. For nine and one-half years the body of Star Trek fandom has twitched reflexively looking for completion. This movie, then, will either be the perfect climax to all that gyrating and increase the popular lust, or, falling short, will invoke Peggy Lee's line: "Is that all there is?" Either way, Star Trek's following will forever change: either be more passionate than ever, or go back to jogging and backgammon. The painter replies: "I don't like to talk dirty so early in the morning."

10:05 a.m.: Robert Wise has called a rehearsal of the principals. De Forest, Bill, Nichelle, Steve, George, and I convene on Stage Ten. The scene we are preparing is the wormhole incident (which, from a physics-astronomy point of view, I still can't get anybody to explain to me) and our imminent collision with an asteroid. It is the sequence scheduled for yesterday that we did not get to. The dialogue is rehearsed with speeches overlapping to create a feeling of urgency.

We go over it several times. Mr. Wise then explains we will shoot the scene in two ways: at the standard 24 frames per second, and then at the slower 48 frames per second. The normal rate is a "back-up" in case the slow-motion effect doesn't look right. The "wormhole" is a time-matter distortion phenomenon which will be a major special effect in the film. We are told that our images will suffer distortion; they will change shape and fragmentize. (It is for this sequence, no doubt, that they are saving my closeup.)

Interesting byplay between Bill and Steve: Decker, who was supposed to be the captain of the newly outfitted *Enterprise* before Kirk was again handed the reins, countermands an order the Captain has given Chekov. To wit: arm photon torpedoes instead of phasers. The scene is written to include Kirk's indecision and chagrin at having given the wrong order. Bill feels that Kirk recovers rapidly and is in charge again only a beat after the crisis has passed. Steve is equally sure that Decker remains in control of the situation for a longer period of time. It is a matter of altering attitude, not dialogue, and I find myself agreeing with Steve.

As I watch them quietly discussing this with our director, I am wondering what part actor ego plays here and what part actor integrity. Is Bill's perspective being colored by his need to be in command (the "star" syndrome), or is his knowledge of Kirk's mind—the military mind with the gears that automatically trip in emergency—dictating his position? The more they discuss the situation, the more patently obvious it is to me that Decker should remain in charge. Furthermore, Robert Wise appears to concur.

Is Bill Shatner succumbing, then, to his own press clippings, so to speak? No sooner have I posed the question to myself than I am feeling guilty for having done so. Just as Bill is the star of this film, so is Kirk the star of the *Enterprise*. The two men are very much interchangeable. Bill has always been so effective as the Captain because he brings so much of himself to the role. To my mind no higher compliment can be paid an actor than to personalize his character, to make the part he plays "organic," an investment of self.

From that perspective it is possible to view any choice that Shatner makes for Kirk as valid for Kirk because it is valid for Shatner. In other words, he is being true to himself, and, by definition, to the part he plays. My point in all this is that if ultimately that choice is invalid for the story, it does not necessarily follow that it was made with an ulterior motive in mind.

As if to wring dry the last drop of cogency from my original conjecture, Bill, on his own, now decides against omnipotence, in favor of human fraility and in agreement with Steve Collins and Robert Wise.

3:07 p.m.: We begin rehearsing the wormhole episode on the set. The first setup will be a master shot. It is an angle we used before, and I can tell immediately that it will not incorporate the weaponry console. However, since the other actors need my lines to respond to, I am asked to assume my chair. I do so happily knowing the afternoon is still young, knowing that it just isn't possible another day could pass without my having worked before the camera.

5:33 p.m.: It is possible. My mood is darker than Chekov's Russian soul as my family arrives to visit and participate in Gene's birthday party later. It is their first time on the set and they are properly impressed. Judy, always with an eye to the esthetic, nods enthusiastically as I take her on the tour. Josh, a science-fiction buff, is absolutely beside himself with all the visual delights. Only my daughter, Danielle, is restrained. In fact, a look sweeps over her face that is somewhere between incredulity, curiosity, and downright terror. She is five and a half and has never before been introduced to a bald-headed female Deltan.

6:20 p.m.: We arrive at Gene's birthday party. It is being held in the *Star Trek* executive offices and it is obvious that there just isn't room for the huge throng already congregated. Eddie Milkis, Robert Justman, and dozens of other old friends from the TV series days are here. Lots of food, lots of warm smiles, and only Walter the grouch to throw a pall over the festivities. Fortunately, everyone is having too good a time to notice.

Robert Wise and his wife, Millicent, leave early. Josh is near the exit as they depart. I introduce him and Josh, totally deadpan, asks if he can have the bridge after shooting is completed. Mr. Wise, equally straight-faced, responds affirmatively. I am awed by the instant rapport between them. I've been on the picture two weeks and would not feel comfortable joking with this quiet, inscrutable man.

After the Wises leave, I look at my son with head atilt. More and more he is evolving into a separate person, stepping out of the shadow of his family and into his own light—a light which, by the way, is very flattering. He is bright, charming, together. On an otherwise bleak afternoon I find something to feel very proud about.

On the other hand, as I am leaving I hand Gene his birthday present (a Big Little Book about Buck Rogers). He takes its graciously and says, "Thank you . . . George."

MONDAY, AUGUST 21

What's worse than finding a wormhole on your sound-stage? Half a wormhole. Technical problems have delayed our progress and we still have little of this sequence on film. Everyone is anxious to push forward. Today, we are promised, we will have the whole of the hole.

8:45 a.m.: On the set, I am curious about the low-key lighting on the bridge. It's very moody and atmospheric and I am wondering what exactly is the message being illuminated here. The speculation culled from several sources ranges from the esthetic to the esoteric. Two weeks in deep space have apparently had an effect on me. On this particular morning, at least, I yearn for dialogue that is more down to earth (like a boiled potato after a binge of gourmet dining—if you'll pardon another metaphor) and opt for the explanation from Darrell Pritchett that the low-key lighting on the actors makes the colorful panel lights on our consoles stand out more. Right on! Nothing like being upstaged by a bunch of light bulbs.

Of course, Darrell's analysis might be a bit self-serving. He is from Paramount's special effects department and is the man responsible for seeing that our consoles operate on cue. He tells me as well that there are approximately sixty 8-mm cassettes and eight projectors for the rear-screened projected images that play across our station "read-out" viewers. Most of these wildly designed and brilliantly colored visuals are mounted on loops so that they can be played over and over again while a scene is in progress. One explanation for the repetition is obvious: our console screens are usually on when there is a degree of jeopardy in the story. We are seeking information. The repetition of that information when it is received makes it seem more important, imbues the situation with a sense of urgency, and ultimately adds to the drama. Another obvious explanation is that it is too costly and time-consuming to do it any other way.

In addition, however, to these "read-out" viewers, there are larger screens at the science and weaponry stations. They register what is happening currently outside the ship (just as does the bridge main viewer). Since this information is story line with a beginning, middle, and an end, it is not on loops but on 16-mm film. "The attack of the giant asteroid" is one such piece of film. It will play on the weaponry console screen when we reach that point in the wormhole encounter. I am anxious to see it.

I decided to calculate the reason it is taking so long to film the wormhole event and I've come up with the following: there are 42 different setups (camera angles) charted for this sequence. Each one is recorded at 24 frames per second and at 48 frames per second. In addition, there are pieces of action being shot on larger 65-mm film (to facilitate optical processing later), as well as on the standard 35-mm. Furthermore, many setups are being recorded on a stable camera, as well as one that is being rocked (to make the *Enterprise* appear to be tossed about). Finally, we are averaging about three attempts (takes) for each time we print a segment of the scene.

A modest estimate would put the number of times these two and a half pages go before the camera at well over 400. Because the bridge lighting is so special and because two objects cannot occupy the same place concurrently, it is not possible to save time by shooting the action with multiple cameras at the same time. The highly sensitive lighting causes shadows to play across actors and instruments that will vary from angle to angle and consequently make unmatchable the same scene as filmed by even contiguous cameras.

No wonder we are in our third day on a scene that will play for about two to three minutes in the final cut of the motion picture.

4:00 p.m.:

> Yesterday upon the stair,
> I met an actor who wasn't there.
> He wasn't there again today,
> I hope tomorrow he'll join the play.

With apologies to the author.

This is the seventh straight day I haven't worked. On four of those occasions I have been called to the studio early and sat in makeup and wardrobe all day without being asked to contribute. All the same, I sense a more benign attitude in myself. Gone is the frustration, the depression, the wish to kill. It's as if I've had a religious experience; I'm feeling very tolerant, at peace with myself.

Que será, será. God will provide.

Mostly, I guess it's self-preservation. To sink deeper into the depths of despair is to risk not being able to get out again and sometime, somewhere down the line Chekov will be called upon, will be required to be bright and shiny for the magic eye. Tomorrow, after all, is another day. Look for the silver lining. Everything good comes to those who wait. Right? Right!

6:15 p.m.: On an impulse I stop by Gene's office on the way home and complain about Chekov's lack of involvement in the film. So much for religious experiences.

TUESDAY, AUGUST 22

The early bird gets caught by the wormhole. So does the late bird. From dawn to dusk the Enterprise *continues its life and death struggle with the forces of nature.*

9:37 a.m.: On the set. Persis, like everyone else, has had some difficulty remembering the technical dialogue. After several false starts she now seems to have it letter-perfect. The shot in progress is close on her as she runs her routine of pushing buttons and swaying and bouncing (as the wormhole draws us in) while giving dramatic value to the confusing polysyllabic terms she is uttering. She's doing it perfectly. Everything is in "sync."

We hold our breath as she approaches the end of her speech: "Impact in seven seconds . . . six . . . five . . . four . . . *two* . . ."

The set breaks up. The entire company is on the floor. Persis is aghast. She sticks her tongue out and, cross-eyed, stares down at it accusingly. Two things about beautiful women: one, even cross-eyed they look beautiful; two, when they make a mistake in their dialogue it's their tongue's fault, not theirs.

There are two special-effects teams working on our project. One group is headed by Alex Weldon and are employees of Paramount Pictures. They are responsible for the effects that do not involve optical printing—in other words, the special "visuals" that are required "live," to be happening in the course of shooting and not in post-production labs. The other group is a company contracted by Paramount to produce the effects that cannot be created on the soundstage. This would include all of the phenomena that occur in space as well as the time-matter distortion experience the crew undergoes. (It is toward this end that the 65-mm camera has been employed. The frame size on 65-mm film is larger than 35-mm and consequently provides more room to accommodate the animation procedures necessary to make the effect work.)

Robert Abel and Associates is the independent company employed by Paramount to achieve these very special visual experiences. They're the ones who did those neat Levi's commercials where the clothing tag bounced along like a pet dog. Not all of their work is post-production, however, and although they are unquestionably very hip, very knowledgeable, and very creative, they are also now very late in producing the effects that are currently scheduled. Paramount has now assigned their own man to oversee their work.

The "opticals" in the film will probably run forty percent of screen time in the finished product. The mass-audience appeal of *Star Wars* and *Close Encounters of the Third Kind* was based in the spectacular special effects employed. It makes me very nervous to hear that we are running into even small problems in this area.

Aside from a few long establishing shots of Vulcan (done in Wyoming), Leonard has not yet worked in the movie. He now comes by in a black Vulcan costume replete with short cape for a film test of the wardrobe. I am suddenly struck by what a sensational Dracula he would make. The perfect vampire! I wonder how he would take such a lefthanded compliment.

11:06 a.m.: Mike Minor, one of the set illustrators, suggests to me that the script might benefit from Chekov's special brand of humor. What a brilliant idea! I can see it now: "The Vormhole was inwented by a liddle ole ladya from Leningrad." Well, maybe not *that* line.

12:12 p.m.: I run into Leonard again on the way to lunch. I begin to tell him that Paramount owns the rights to the novel *Interview with a Vampire,* but he anticipates me. He's been talking to them for over a year and a half about the project with nothing resolved as yet. I guess an actor is an actor is an actor, and a good role, even if it's the living dead with pale skin, red eyes, and long teeth, is an attractive prospect.

2:20 p.m.: All things come to those who wait. The camera at last and my immortal lines: "Photon torpedoes armed . . . targeting asteroid . . . torpedoes away."

This first angle is a master shot past Decker and Chekov (he has rushed to the Russian's side to belay Kirk's order for phasers) and encompassing most of the bridge. In order to get it they have had to take out the wall behind my console and shoot into the bridge from offstage. It's the first time we have done this and it points up a problem that the director and cinematographer must contend with. Not only must the story line progress and the characters grow and evolve during the course of the film, but the moving pictures recording these elements must also remain interesting to look at. It is not such a big problem when you are shooting a predominantly "exterior" story or even one where you have a host of interior sets that you can jump between. It is indeed a problem when one set dominates in your picture and you must return again and again to it. I would guess that nearly fifty percent of the movie will be shot on the bridge. It becomes imperative, therefore, to keep the tableau from becoming stagnant by finding fresh ways to shoot the action. This current setup would appear to be a perfect example.

2:55 p.m.: We continue to rehearse from this angle. At this point in the plot the asteroid has been pulled into the wormhole with us and we are on a collision course. At the same time we are being sucked deeper and deeper into the vortex. The deeper we are driven, the more we jiggle, bump, shake, rattle, and roll. While this is happening, I am trying to reach the button to fire the torpedo to destroy the asteroid. Since all the bouncing around is self-induced, I am expending considerable energy pushing myself away from the panel while straining with the rest of my strength to reach it. It's sort of like an isometric exercise, the kind you're suppose to do for thirty seconds at a time. It's now been thirty-five minutes.

6:30 p.m.: We finally get the master shot and then set up for another angle of the same business. We do it again and again and again and then shoot still another setup of this sequence. In all, I work four hours and ten minutes trying to fire the bloody torpedoes. The lights are intensely hot and I'm drenched and exhausted. We'll do it all over again tomorrow, probably most of the day. My screen time for this scene in the finished picture may be four or five seconds long. But you know what? I love every second of the fifteen thousand we've spent on it so far. An actor is an actor is an actor, indeed.

6:45 p.m.: I'm heading for my car and am stopped by two nineteen-year-old girls who have come down from Winnipeg expressly to meet Bill Shatner. Despite the foreknowledge that there would be guards stationed at all the entrances to the studio and that *Star Trek* was a "closed set" production, they have managed to slip onto the lot and make their way to our soundstage.

They are momentarily crushed when I explain that Bill has left for the day but bounce back with fresh resolve to try again tomorrow. I know they will have greater difficulty slipping past security during the daylight hours. They are apparently willing to risk the consequence of trying. I admire their tenacity. Too many people go through life lukewarm. I am always impressed by people with passion, the cause notwithstanding. Homage must be paid. I tell them that if they are in front of the studio at the corner of Gower and Melrose at 7:15 tomorrow morning, they can drive on with me.

WEDNESDAY, AUGUST 23

The wormhole turns . . . and turns . . . and turns as the Enterprise *continues to spin deeper into its black heart.*

7:33 a.m.: The Winnipeg girls are waiting as promised. I drive them into the studio, passing them off as my nieces. We part inside the gates as I wish them luck in their quest to see Bill.

8:05 a.m.: Makeup room. Most of us are congregated here now, getting our makeup applied. The results always amaze me. Ponce de Leon should have forgotten about Florida and headed for Paramount. The conversation this morning is again about the wormhole. It is definitely becoming a catch phrase. Everyone tries to top each other with dreadful puns using the term. **I,** of course, abstain from this wormholier-than-thou stuff.

A twenty-foot-by-forty-foot bank of fluorescent lights has been erected outside the bridge in line with the main viewscreen. A blue scrim, the dimensions of this illuminated wall, is stretched over it. It thus becomes the "blue screen" referred to in the lexicon when there is optical printing to be done. For our purposes it represents space.

When the main viewer screen is not in place and we are at our posts on the bridge, we are looking out directly into the blue screen. Frequently, the camera is positioned behind the actors, shooting past their backs out toward the ship exterior. This is done to establish actors and space in the same shot. Since we do not have deep space available to us on the soundstage, the wall of lights is erected in its place. However, the blue screen will not appear in the finished picture. It is there primarily to establish mat lines for the animation effects that will be introduced later. The blue color is used because it is relatively easy to chemically separate out that color from the film without affecting whatever else is going on (the actor's images, for example) in the film frame.

It is for the purpose of these mat shots that the 65-mm camera is employed by Abel and Associates. The wider the film frame, the more room to mat in the optical detail in the lab. Of course, once accomplished, the 65-mm picture will be transferred back to 35-mm for viewing in movie theaters.

2:37 p.m.: I learn that the girls from Winnipeg finally caught up with Bill. When he first met them he feigned irritation, telling them to go back to Canada where they came from. (Bill is, of course, Canadian.) He then got someone to move them—each time disguised in a different alien head appliance—from one location on the soundstage to another with the dire warning on each occasion that they must remain absolutely still until someone else came for them. In the course of their journey through the soundstage, they had visited every set, ending up, finally, standing frozen on the transporter platform ready to be beamed away. Alas, the experience by now had so unnerved them they failed to appreciate that they had been where no fan had gone before. Ultimately, Bill sat down with them in his dressing room and they all had a long chat together.

On the way out they thanked me profusely for my assistance in their adventure. It was quite apparent that it had been all very much worthwhile.

5:55 p.m.: The rest of the afternoon is spent bouncing, bouncing, bouncing. I'm not sure that this is why I spent two years in the Neighborhood Playhouse drama school living on seventy-five dollars a month, but I'm ecstatic all the same.

6:25 p.m.: They've decided to show dailies after work instead of at noon. I love the master shot of the bridge with the silhouettes of Steve and myself in the foreground. It gives the set a whole new spectacular look. On the other hand, I can't decide how to react to the two shots of Decker and Chekov. I finally conclude that the best thing to do is not react at all. In my all-shook-up state halfway to exhaustion, that's not hard to do.

8:00 p.m.: Persis's party at Gypsies, the East Indian restaurant. We take over the place, filling up all three rooms with the thirty people she has invited. The food is spicy but very good. Despite my fatigue, a very pleasant evening. Thank you, Persis.

THURSDAY, AUGUST 24

The asteroid is destroyed (I think there is a song there) and the indomitable crew of the Enterprise *is again safe. (Did you doubt?) With the danger past, Kirk, Decker, and McCoy withdraw from the bridge to discuss further Decker's countermanding of Kirk's phaser order.*

8:52 a.m.: The makeup room. George has a laugh that sounds like something between a jammed Tommy gun and a seal in heat. Ve Neill, one of the makeup artists, has the maniacal giggle that Richard Widmark made famous when he threw the old lady down the stairs in *Kiss of Death.* Each one's chortle is most amusing to the other, and before long a dozen other people are laughing at George and Ve laughing at each other. The mass hysterics go on for many minutes, getting louder and louder with each tick of the padded clock. The inmates have overrun the asylum! It's bonkers in Bedlam!

Little-known facts about the *Star Trek* production: *One:* the armrests on the bridge chairs fold in to become restraints so that under attack we don't fall out of our seats. Four of these chairs are electronically operated and open and close by the push of a button. The others close manually. The trouble is that one of the manual chairs flies open when the actor bounces around vigorously inside it. To keep it closed, in this fifteen-million-dollar production, ordinary cloth tape is jerry-rigged between the armrests across the actor's lap. *Two:* one of the time-consuming problems having to be dealt with is light bouncing off set pieces and reflecting into the camera. The solution to the offending shine is Nestlé's Streaks and Tips brown hair spray. *Three:* the life-support belts worn by the bridge crew have had to be replaced three times. The problem is that when we jiggle up and down (*i.e.*, the wormhole), the belts rub against the consoles and the paint becomes scratched on the surface of the buckle. *Four:* Remember the trouble with the special effects in the malfunctioning transporter? It's still malfunctioning. In order to escape running into yet another day's shooting in there, Robert Abel's crew is filming in the transporter while Robert Wise continues to shoot on the bridge. What is unusual about this is that two different crews are shooting two different scenes at the same time on the same soundstage. I've never run into that before. *Five:* Paramount has ordered that the powdered chicken soup for afternoon snacking be discontinued. This, of course, is tantamount to withholding quinine from malaria victims.

6:20 p.m.: We've done it! We're out of the wormhole! Kirk, McCoy, and Decker have departed, Sulu has the conn, and Chekov has definitely been established as a member of the crew. So ends the fourteenth day of production on the *Star Trek* movie.

6:35 p.m.: Paramount has a policy of running periodic checks on the contents of all cars leaving the studio lot. No one is exempted from this procedure, not even the top-echelon employees. Today is such a day, and now I know I truly belong. On the way out the guard asks me to open my trunk to see if I've stolen anything.

FRIDAY, AUGUST 26

Mr. Spock comes aboard the Enterprise *for the first time. It is* Dr. Chapel's *initial visit to the bridge as well.*

8:52 a.m.: Up until now we've worked only on Stage Nine. For the first scene of the day, however, we have moved over to Stage Seventeen. Someone is coming aboard the *Enterprise* via shuttlecraft. Chekov, as head of security, has been ordered to meet the ship's unidentified passenger at the command airlock pod hatch. While waiting I exchange a brief greeting with one of the security guards in my charge who is posted at the pod entrance. The man is huge. I am again put in mind of *Of Mice and Men,* only this time (see how versatile I am?) I'm George, not Lennie.

Leonard steps through the sliding doors dressed in his black Vulcan garb. Chekov is surprised and excited. He tries to express his enthusiasm at seeing Spock again, but the Vulcan cuts him short with a perfunctory salutation and steps past him. Same old Mr. Spock!

9:19 a.m.: An actor friend of mine visits with a vengeance. He criticizes everything he sees. I begin to realize how enviable it is to be working on this film.

10:37 a.m.: We have finished the three quick setups of Spock's entrance and now we're back on Nine and back on the bridge.

Ilia does a tongue trip on one of her lines. Instead of "intersecting course," it comes out "sex intercoursing."

While waiting to be called, I thumb through the script and confirm a suspicion I've had. Due to a story quirk, if they continue to shoot in sequence I will not work with Jimmy Doohan until the last week of production. Ensconced in engineering, he doesn't appear on the bridge until the "tag." As far as I can recall, the only time that Chekov ever had a personal dialogue with Scotty in the TV series was in the "Tribbles" episode. (I'm sure there are a countless number of "Star

Trek" devotees out there who can cite chapter and verse in rebuttal to the foregoing.) It doesn't appear as if that situation will be corrected here. Too bad; on that one occasion at least, I did very much enjoy working with that fine actor. In any event, aside from the photo session we've had, I haven't seen him at all. I wonder how he must feel waiting so long for his scenes to finally begin shooting. Or is it just me that goes so totally berserk when I'm not working?

12:00 p.m.: Dailies. The *Star Trek* movie is being shot with an anamorphic lens that squeezes the image to one-half its normal width. This is done in order to get more picture in each film frame. Another anamorphic lens is used on the projector to convert the image back to its proper proportions.

As we watch the dailies now, some of the sequences appear to have a slightly soft focus. I'm not even aware of it until it is pointed out, but in a production of this magnitude in which so much care is otherwise taken, the modest focus problem becomes a major source of concern. To determine whether it is the lens on the camera or the lens on the projector that is causing the fuzziness, the film is shown again with a lens that does not convert the images to their proper proportions. As a result, we suddenly all now look very tall and slim, which would be highly flattering if our heads didn't also suddenly all now look very tall and slim.

No definitive conclusion is arrived at, and for the first time I hear evidence of temper. Robert Wise flares briefly. It amounts to nothing more than raising his voice a single decibel, but from so quiet a man it sounds like the rages of Hell to me. I make a mental note to sink my incisors deep into my tongue should I be seized again with the impulse to help him direct this picture.

1:00 p.m.: A decision has been made to change Panavision cameras. It is hoped that doing so will remedy the focus problem.

1:55 p.m.: I had forgotten what a quick wit Bill possesses. George and I are having a discussion about the meaning of the word "demagogue"—whether inferred in its meaning is the quality of proselytism. Bill passes by and without missing a step postulates that if a demagogue is one who is bent on conversion, then a demagogue who promotes naughty things must be a *sin* agogue.

2:33 p.m.: I think I've discovered an interesting thing about Robert Wise. If his present disposition is any indication, it would appear that anger does not sustain in him. He seems able to shake it off at will and get on with the business at hand. I am very impressed. The sign of an inordinately mature man. I'm even tempted to help him direct again.

Working for Robert Wise has been edifying in an artistic way, too. I have in the past found it discouraging to go through the arduous process of preparing for a difficult scene and then having what I consider my best take spoiled by one of a host of problems that I have no control over. The complexity of this project, however, dictates shooting each sequence many, many times. Knowing that going in, I find that I am less inclined to hold any performance of mine too preciously. The odds are it is going to be redone. I am predisposed to accept that and consequently predisposed not to fret if a good take for me is not a good one for the people behind the camera. The effect of all this is that I'm more relaxed, which, in turn, gives me more freedom of self and more spontaneity in the succeeding efforts. As a result, each time we shoot I am able to respond with a degree of truthfulness I had reached far less frequently in the TV series.

5:11 p.m.: We have begun rehearsing Spock's entrance onto the bridge. This scene also marks Majel Barrett's introduction to the project. She is supposed to step out of the elevator with De Forest and be joyously startled to see Mr. Spock again. When the elevator doors open for the first rehearsal, however, she and De are engaged in a fierce embrace. Everybody breaks up. Time and space do not exist. It's the old days all over again. Welcome to *Star Trek*.

6:20 p.m.: The third week is over. We now have twenty-one pages of story in the can. If we were to continue at this pace, production would wrap December 9. More than three months more to film *Star Trek—The Motion Picture*. The battle is still before us.

MONDAY, AUGUST 28

Together again for the first time! Spock and Chapel on film in the brand-new Star Trek—The Motion Picture *motion picture!! At least that's the plan for today.*

8:45 a.m.: I have learned the real reason for the mood lighting on the bridge. It establishes an atmosphere of reality. The sense of it is that the lighting is functional to the ship rather than accommodating to the audience. People watching the film will feel less like invited spectators and more like stowaways participating in the action. The genius of the lighting design (and its effectiveness cannot be minimized) is that it totally conveys this feeling while still lighting everyone appropriately. Richard Kline, our cinematographer, with the sanction of our director, is responsible for this new "look" aboard the *Enterprise*.

It is also true, but perhaps only as an effect of the primary reason, that the subtle bridge lighting will contrast very effectively with the colorful and intense pyrotechnic light displays planned for events yet to transpire on the bridge.

10:25 a.m.: I learn that the scene in which I am burned (remember the sickbay wardrobe?) is to take place on Wednesday. I am measured for a perforated copper tube that will fit around my waist. I am told that by means of a hose, propane gas will be pumped through the tube. Just before the camera rolls, the gas will be ignited and flames will shoot up my back. It sounds terrific . . . I think. I am escorted to Stage Seventeen and given a demonstration as to how it will work. Alex Weldon, the special effects foreman, is himself the subject. His only protection is a pad of asbestos between his body and the copper tubing. The gas is pumped and ignited with a lighter. It sure looks effective—particularly when the fire continues to run up Alex's back for ten seconds after the gas valve is shut off. They finally have to extinguish the flames with a blanket. I love Alex. He always has a big "hello" and a smile for everyone, but if this little demonstration was supposed to reassure me, somebody has miscalculated.

It seems like *Star Trek* has practically taken over the studio. In addition to Stage Nine (bridge, etc.), Stage Ten (makeup, rehearsals, wardrobe storage), and Stage Seventeen (pod hatch), other sets remain to be built on Stages Six and Fifteen. In addition, outdoor space has been slotted to our company for the construction of our one principal exterior set. To top all that off, the entire inside of Stage Eight is currently being converted into the *Enterprise* Rec Deck. Stage Eight connects with Stage Nine, and each day as I come to work I peek in to see how far they have progressed. Unlike a real building where the work is accomplished so slowly that you are not aware of the changes occurring, the work here is like the stop-action photography of a flower opening. Each morning it has grown bigger, more imposing, more beautiful. Yes, I admit it, I'm a closet freak for the Rec Deck.

Fans are always asking about our complement of 400 and the fact that they hardly ever see any of the *Enterprise* crew with the exception of the regulars and an occasional expendable security officer. Well, you want to see crew members, we'll give you crew members! The plan at this time is to bring in 300 people (including assorted aliens) to staff the rec hall when it finally goes before the cameras. "Ready when you are, C.B."

12:24 p.m.: Dailies. The focus problem has apparently been corrected. Everyone seems happy with the new Panavision camera brought in Friday afternoon. I get a chance to see my pod-hatch scene with Spock. It's very short but okay. I even like the way I look. I start to breathe a sigh of relief when I realize that this could be an expendable scene. If the picture runs long it could easily be cut. What's the name of that character in "L'il Abner" who is forever fated to walk beneath a gray cloud?

They are talking about the finished picture running two hours and ten minutes. The uneven length is not arbitrary. Any longer than that and the theater owners become faced with either stretching their screening day or lopping one showing of the film from their program.

The script currently runs 132 pages, and at an average of about one minute per page, they are right on pace.

3:35 p.m.: Dick Rubin, the property master, tells me that Robert Wise and Gene Roddenberry are having second thoughts about the burning sequence. I can't, however, get a definitive report as to what alternatives are being considered. Being the only character who gets burned and survives may be my mark of distinction in the film. On the other hand, being the only *actor* in this film who gets burned and doesn't survive is a possibility, too. What to do? What to do? Celluloid survival or cellular survival? Roll the cameras!

4:11 p.m.: I've just been told that Paramount has raised the budget on our little opus to twenty-four million dollars. Maybe now they'll give us back our dried chicken soup.

5:08 p.m.: They are shooting the closeup on Kirk as he reacts to Spock's very cold, very detached first meeting with our crew. I'm off camera but close by for a line that the Captain addresses to Chekov. I'm therefore carefully watching Kirk as he reacts first with surprise and joy at Spock's entrance and then love, hurt, and finally anger as the enigmatic Vulcan rejects the camaraderie that once bound these two so closely together. In my heart of hearts I've always considered myself—at my best, in the right part—as good an actor as any in this production, but I'm truly awed by Bill's performance here. His total involvement, the vulnerability he permits himself, the honesty of this moment for him are the performance qualities of a truly fine talent. This small, silent closeup on him becomes the perfect match of filmic technique and organic behavior, and I applaud him the achievement.

5:52 p.m.: Bulova watch time. The word is passed around that Bulova has made a deal with Paramount to produce a watch that looks like our new wrist communicators. Like many such stories, I can't get anyone to confirm it, but I love the concept. As a child I had the psychological orientation of a pack rat. I was a compulsive horder who collected everything: bubblegum cards, marbles, pinback buttons, comic books, bottle caps, lead soldiers, comic figurines; the list goes on and on. The first time as an adult (I use the term loosely) that I saw myself (Chekov) on a bubble-gum card I grew absolutely giddy. The first time I saw myself in a comic book I was convinced that I was moving at 186,000 miles per second and proving Einstein's theory, only better. Not only had I gone back in time, but I was fulfilling my childhood fantasies; I was the super hero of my own daydreams! In time, Koenig-Chekov appeared on pinback buttons and toy boxes. All that was missing from this cornucopia of ego strokes was the three-dimensional toy itself; there had never been a Chekov doll! The Bulova-*Star Trek* deal sets me to contemplate the enormous merchandising that will undoubtedly take place when the picture is released. More bubble-gum cards, more comic books, more buttons, more toys, and maybe this time, this time my rightful place among the world's great icons.

6:27 p.m.: After again studying Friday's dailies shot with the new Panavision camera, it is now conclusively determined that the focus problem may or may not have been caused by things known or unknown and may or may not now be remedied.

TUESDAY, AUGUST 29

We're still reacting to Spock's entrance. We resume warp drive without incident. (It was our anti-matter imbalance caused by our push toward warp drive that created the wormhole (whatever that is) in the first place. We begin rehearsing the next scene, a red alert in which the alien force we've been sent to stop approaches for the first time.

8:15 a.m.: The hip-hugging copper manifold has been perfected. The highly combustible propane gas will be pumped through tubing at one end and set afire while I writhe in pretend agony inside my asbestos padding. To extinguish the flames, helium gas will be pumped through tubing at the other end. I watch a demonstration. It works perfectly and on cue. I can have my bake and cheat it, too.

8:45 a.m.: We get our first shot. It's a two-shot of Uhura and Chekov reacting to the interplay between Kirk and Spock filmed yesterday. The successful take is cause for a modest celebration. It is the earliest we have ever recorded a print.

10:11 a.m.: A conference is called: Gene Roddenberry, Robert Wise, Alex Weldon, Fred Phillips, William Mas (costumer), Dick Rubin, and Chekov. They have decided not to use the manifold, after all. Only the Russian's hand and arm will get burned. I assume that the shot will be too close on me to use a stunt double and they are being motivated by concern for my safety. Bless them. The less elaborate effect does not, however, eliminate the problems. My arm is very hairy. It will be difficult to cover with the burn makeup envisioned. The solution arrived at: change my blouse from the Class-A (formal attire) to the Reuben top. The former is a wool gabardine that won't show a heat effect, while the latter, a polyester, will blacken and melt when ignited. The shirt will be burned before I put it on. Since it is long-sleeved, only the melted sleeve and not my arm will show. Since my hirsute limb will not be revealed, makeup need be applied only to my scorched hand. Clever, these Federationalists.

3:12 p.m.: An elaborate camera rig has been created for an inordinately complex camera sweep of the bridge. Eight feet above the deck a squared rail structure hangs suspended from vertical metal rods attached above the set at the catwalk. In the middle of this structure, running the distance between the north-south rails and perpendicular to them, is another track that contacts the rails by means of a wheel at each end. Hanging down from this center track and also connected by a wheel is an accordion-shaped apparatus (a scissors hinge) borrowed from a hospital X-ray machine. Attached to this scissors hinge is a swivel, and suspended about four and a half feet above the ground from the swivel is the camera. Thus rigged, the camera can be rotated 360 degrees (on the swivel), can be moved up and down (on the scissors hinge), can be moved east and west, (on the connected wheel along the east-west track), and can be moved north-south by means of the wheeled middle track along the north-south sides of the rail structure. With this flexibility, not only can all moves be made steadily, but they can be made simultaneously. It is employed to capture the various reactions of the crew at their stations as the *Enterprise* energizes past warp one on its way to warp seven.

There is considerable tension here since the last time we revved the engines we ended up in a wormhole jeopardy. The camera moving steadily, relentlessly, augments the tension of the crew as the ship steadily, relentlessly, gains speed. After the predictable difficulties getting everything to work in unison, the sequence comes together. Everyone seems quite pleased with the results. I look forward to seeing it in tomorrow's dailies.

3:35 p.m.: We retire to Stage Ten for a rehearsal of the "red alert" scene. Questions, comments, concepts fly thick and fast. Steve is concerned about his character, Bill is concerned about his character, Leonard is concerned about his character. Robert Wise is concerned about everybody's character.

Bill wants to juxtapose speeches in a way that would change the thrust of the sequence from a conflict between him and Decker to a conflict with himself. Steve feels that if this is done, Decker becomes just one of several hostile stimuli to the Captain instead of his principal antagonist in the scene. He doesn't feel that's right.

Leonard is concerned that Spock's dialogue as written makes the character appear unsure. He volunteers lines that imbue the Vulcan with greater confidence.

I can see merit in all the suggestions. Certainly, Bill's changes would make the Captain's turmoil more interesting, and Leonard's contribution would appear to be consistent with the character he portrayed on the television series. But I'm wondering as well whether the dramatic thrust of the scene might be thrown off balance were it played as Bill would like it played and whether Leonard's new lines might not be illogical (God forgive me) based on the very limited knowledge of the current situation that Spock has in the story.

4:48 p.m.: Over the course of several rehearsals at the table on Stage Ten and now back on the set, subtle adjustments are made, nuances added. When the camera finally does roll, Steve plays the scene more authoritatively, forcing a more equitable balance of power between Decker and Kirk; Bill maintains the Captain's inner turmoil while respecting the conflict between the two ranking officers; and Leonard adds a note of conjecture to his speech that changes an omniscient attitude to one of supposition based on calculated probability. Robert Wise is satisfied, harmony has been maintained, professionalism reigns. To top it all off, we get the shot in one take. And they all lived happily ever after. . . .

4:54 p.m.: Nichelle has wanted a phone in her dressing room. She is now told by Phil Rawlins, the unit production manager, that it is not practical because those of us relegated to the bridge (Nichelle, George, and me) have only fourteen days left on the movie. She relays the information and I am immediately disconsolate. My first thought is to my bank account, but on the heels of that, I suddenly realize how much I will genuinely miss being here. The depression of the first week or so has long ago lifted. In its place is a satisfying "high" that endures day after day. The *Star Trek* set is my Shangri-La. With the darkened sideburns and five inches of makeup, I am, when viewed squinty-eyed, ten years younger. It is still the 1960s. Nixon isn't yet President, flower children are a fresh memory, my property tax is still bearable. On many, not all, surely, but on many counts, a time of hope and promise for a better tomorrow. And now, quite abruptly, it seems to me, it's going to end.

6:35 p.m.: We wrap for the day. I walk out into the cold gray evening checking my hands for liver spots.

WEDNESDAY, AUGUST 30

"Red alert! Red alert!" No, that isn't a wake-up call for a sleeping Russian lieutenant; it's what the Russian lieutenant gets to say when the ship's formidable adversary starts ringing the chimes at the front door.

11:21 a.m.: Rehearsal: "There is an object in the center of the cloud," says Mr. Spock.

"Object in the *heart* of the cloud," corrects Bonnie Prendergast, the script supervisor.

Leonard listens impassively.

New rehearsal: Mr. Spock turned toward the Captain:

"There is an object in the liver of the cloud."

Kirk whirls on him: "You have the guts to tell me that?!"

Everyone roars. We're falling further behind in our shooting schedule, but we're having fun doing it.

11:50 a.m.: Jimmy Doohan stops by. A lot of warm smiles all around. Our family isn't quite complete without the Scotsman. He is supposed to participate in some tests of the engine room tomorrow afternoon but is not scheduled to start work for still another week.

12:30 p.m.: Jimmy and I go to lunch together and discuss among other things the upcoming Labor Day weekend convention in New York. At last we can tell the big crowds about a Star Trek that is current, that is happening now. No more ghosts, no more spirits of Christmas past.

There are 2,500 handmade parts in the engine, I am informed. I don't really understand why we can't just lift off the soundstage and assume our rightful place among the stars.

3:00 p.m.: We are handed a shooting schedule for the rest of the production. I note that my last day is October 26. That's eight weeks away, not fourteen days! The butler has confessed, the governor has called at the twelfth hour, I've been reprieved!

6:11 p.m.: Nichelle gets her phone.

12:05 a.m.: Literary allusion gives way to literal fact. This afternoon's figurative "stay of execution" has a real-life counterpart. I've been tossing and turning in my bed for two hours. Somewhere in the public park close by, the sounds of The Grateful Dead blast full volume on a radio. The band's moniker reflects accurately my sanguinary frame of mind.

Clad in pajamas and primed to an emotional pitch (the only way I can force myself out into the ominous dark), I make my way toward the cacophonous source. The radio, I discover, plays inside a vacant truck parked at the curb paralleling the park. I scream every conceivable epithet but cannot be heard above the din. Frustrated beyond restraint, I reach in and shut off the radio.

A cry, probably human, but sounding like a wounded but definitely ambulatory Gorillacus Violenticus, now challenges me from the recesses of the wooded plain. Terrified but feeling homicidal nevertheless, I advance at a gallop toward the unseen enemy. Advance, that is, until the target of my fury rises from the tall grass and makes itself visible. Three huge silhouettes hulk toward me, dragging arms that in my palpable fear seem to extend to the ground and furrow the earth as they move. I am convinced my hour of reckoning has come and that I will not again see the light of day. To be sure, were it not for the light of night, a glorious full moon, the prophecy might well have had substance. The moon, sifting through the trees, has apparently bathed my twitching countenance in its pale beam, for the adversary, a few scant feet away, now suddenly halts. I can see clearly the face of the leader as the lantern jaw falls away and a flash of recognition lights the otherwise dim psychopathic eyes. He drops into a crouch, whips his hand across his hip, and produces an imaginary weapon that he aims (index finger and thumb) at my heart. "Phasers on stun!" he screams, and then is beside himself with laughter as my already boneless limbs turn completely to gelatin.

Twice in one day I have been reprieved, twice in one day *Star Trek* has come to my rescue.

They are still giggling maniacally as I squish-squash on unsubstantial props back to my home. "Good night, Mr. Chekov" are the last words I hear as I shut and double-lock the door behind me.

THURSDAY, AUGUST 31

Wherein we discover that the cloud-shaped entity has an out-of-this-universe strength.

10:09 a.m.: Jesco von Puttkamer, the technical advisor to the *S.T.* project and our man at NASA, has been visiting all week. Having received satisfaction nowhere else, I now ask him what a wormhole is supposed to be. According to his explanation, it is a black hole that moves like a whirlpool. Only after he has departed does it occur to me to wonder how our anti-matter imbalance could have *caused* the wormhole when one presumes that black holes and whirlpooling black holes exist independently of starships. After all, black holes are a scientific reality, and our *Enterprise,* despite my flights of fantasy, is not.

We are well past wormholes, however, and are now concentrating on another danger: an enemy with a twelfth-power energy field and dimensions so immense that next to it the *Enterprise* becomes a microscopic dot. As with the wormhole, there will be a host of special effects here—effects that have been diagramed but not yet realized.

4:00 p.m.: We are still shooting scenes leading up to our confrontation with the omnipotent enemy when it is announced that Friday will be a day off for all the actors and that the following two weeks will be devoted to shooting scenes in the engine room. Abel and Associates need time to implement their effects concept for the impending bridge attack and resultant conflagration the adversary causes, and Robert Wise would, in any event, like some time off from the bridge. I can only guess that it is as taxing as it appears to continually maintain a fresh approach for the nearly four straight weeks of shooting he has directed in the claustrophobic, self-contained environment of the bridge set.

This is still the age of "cool," I am discovering. Some of my peers on the film have assumed a somewhat cynical posture. "Take the money and run" seems to be the prevailing stance. Not the same, I feel, as the concern for my wallet I expressed earlier when I believed my days on the project were down to a precious few. Different because, despite the façade of mercenary detachment, I don't believe *them.* Me, I really am greedy about the windfall this movie is providing and at the same time rejoice in the opportunity to be part of this production. They, I don't think the money is *that* important, but rather than admitting to a frequent euphoric rush, to an occasional giddy lightheadedness, to a once-in-a-blue-moon heavy spontaneous trip in recreating their characters, they affect the cynicism of the world-weary and profess that it is the bucks that count. Baloney! The glacial age is again upon us.

4:52 p.m.: Since today is Thursday and the cloud-shaped entity has not yet sent its (animated) energy bolts flying across our bridge, I have not yet been burned. Obviously, my auto de fé originally scheduled for yesterday is still sometime off. I am now informed by Alex's crew that a new idea has been proposed for toasting my epidermis. The few minor kinks in it, I'm assured, will be ironed out during the hiatus. *Kinks,* did they say?

September

SATURDAY, SUNDAY, MONDAY, SEPTEMBER 2-4

The New York Labor Day convention. Several things to be noted.

One: the crowds are bigger and more enthusiastic than the S.T. con last February and the preceding Labor Day convention. I sense from the fans that they are no longer exhuming the past but rallying around the future.

Two: I'm told that I've never appeared so relaxed, so loose, in front of the large gatherings as I do now. I haven't been aware of it, but in retrospect I know it's true. For the first time I needn't feel self-conscious about discussing Star Trek or the character of Chekov. This time, after nearly ten years, there is a new and fresh Star Trek, not an after-image and a warm-bodied, button-pushing Russian, not a spook.

Three: I ask Isaac Asimov to explain the wormhole phenomenon to me and how it would relate to an anti-matter imbalance. Before he is dragged away by adoring fans, he tells me that the wormhole concept is theory, not fact, and currently is in disfavor among some physicists. That's not what I asked him.

Four: The T-shirt I like best at the con is the one with the familiar line: "He's dead, Jim."

Five: A nearsighted matron requests a kiss on the cheek but somehow misses the runway completely and does a thirty-two-point landing that envelops my nose. I am envisioning the headline "ACTOR BITTEN TO DEATH" when she finally extricates her molars from around my proboscis.

Six: The September 4 issue of Time *Magazine I read at the con postulates in its Science section that wormholes may be passages in "rapidly rotating black holes" through which matter can be moved through time and space to "re-emerge in a different part of the universe or perhaps in another universe entirely." My God, is* that *what almost happened to us? No wonder Chekov was so scared.*

Seven: Several times I am asked, "What was it really like playing on 'Star Trek' . . . George?"

THURSDAY, SEPTEMBER 14

It is Bilbo's, Frodo's, and Walter's birthday. My wife throws a small party. The other two celebrants don't attend but some of my non-Star Trek friends do. I am asked whatever happened to that Star Trek *movie they were planning: Did it ever get off the ground? I am surprised. But I am not surprised by my surprise. What I had suspected might happen has indeed occurred. Insulated away from the real world by my involvement with the Paramount production, I had forgotten the possibility that there might be people "out there" not terribly interested in the* Star Trek *enterprise. A couple of my guests are living proof. Of course, I make a mental note never to invite them to my house again.*

MONDAY, SEPTEMBER 18

Back on the bridge, back being pursued by the entity. Today we start dodging the whiplash energy bolts it fires at us.

9:27 a.m.: "Battlestar Galactica" was launched on television last night. I found myself involuntarily making comparisons. As best I could, however, I attempted to withhold judgment until I had a night's sleep under my lids. The conclusions I've reached this morning as I wait for our own film to get rolling again are: one— the show is fun in the way *Star Wars* was fun; two—it is not innovative, particularly after *Star Wars;* three— its most spectacular element is, by nature of the medium, self-defeating. The vastness of space is belittled by the smallness of the tube, and consequently the dogfight pyrotechnics become more a detached observation for the viewer than an enveloping experience.

At the time of the "Star Trek" television series, special effects and the money for them were not available to us in such lavish quantity. Although Gene's main thrust for the series had always been character and story, in the absence of highly elaborate "optics" we perhaps concentrated even more in those areas. Testament to our success is that now, almost ten years later, there has still been nothing in episodic science-fiction TV to compare with the overall quality of our product.

Now, however, in addition to the creative writing elements, we have the budget, the technical expertise, and the canvas to do a space story properly in all its dimensions. Even as I sit here in my dressing room impatiently waiting out yet another delay, I am convinced that *Star Trek* on the big screen will again sprint to the head of the field.

I am anxious to poll my co-workers for their reactions to "Battlestar." After all, is it possible that my attitude is simply one of wishful thinking? Perhaps the weight of their opinions will answer my question.

11:15 a.m.: There is a new piece of equipment on the soundstage. It is called a chem editing table and functions as a sophisticated Moviola®. It runs 35-mm film on one reel and magnetic sound tape on another to show footage previously shot. It is being used as a guidepost for recreating the bridge scenes (*i.e.,* their composition) that were considered "soft" earlier and that will now be redone.

We hover around it watching our images flick by. Unlike the dailies, the sequences here have already been edited. They appear in order with the appropriate cuts to the different angles included. It looks very much as it will in the finished motion picture. The running time for this piece is perhaps twenty seconds, but it is the first time we have seen any segment of the film strung together and we are all a bit excited. It lives, it breathes, it walks, it talks!

Speaking of new: we have a new wardrobe man and a new makeup man. Speaking of soft: security on the set has been tightened. A benign attitude has resulted in too many people visiting. Hereafter, all guests will be required to wear badges. Speaking of recreating: Paramount has given us back our dried chicken soup.

Changes always make me feel a trifle unsettled. What next? "Mr. Koenig, we would like you to do the rest of Chekov's lines with a slightly Swedish accent."

Quotes on "Battlestar Galactica":

BILL—"It was a lot of fun."

ANONYMOUS—"It sucks."

NICHELLE—"They did borrow from every science-fiction movie ever made, didn't they?"

GEORGE—"We have met the competition and we are victorious." [And he didn't even know I was going to quote him.]

LEONARD—"I didn't see it."

3:23 p.m.: The retakes have been completed and we now retire to Stage Ten for rehearsal of the next installment of our encounter with the adversary.

There seems to be an inordinate concern about lines that refer to the ship's yaw and pitch. "Yaw 60 degrees to port, 40-degree negative pitch" is the written line that seems to be at the center of the discussion. Several of the crew need to be standing when this reading is made and it is questionable that they will be able to maintain balance and carry out their duties with the *Enterprise,* supposedly, in such a severe attitude. Back and forth, back and forth the conversation yaws and pitches. "Well, if we changed it to 30-degree pitch and 40-degree yaw . . ." "On the other hand, it's not the yaw at all . . ." "If the pitch were positive . . ." "I'm sure we can get away with a 30-degree negative pitch . . ." "Let's split the difference: 37-degree negative pitch, 40-degree yaw . . ." "But it isn't the yaw . . ." I am fascinated by the intense concentration and energy brought to bear in this five-sided discussion.

To a point there is logic in what they are trying to accomplish. Beyond that point the whole thing sounds as inconsequential to me as it is consuming to those at the table. "A 45-degree negative pitch is half of a 90-degree angle. . . ." [Zounds!] "If the ship is yawing to port, then wouldn't the pitch be backward . . . ?" I'm beginning to think *I'm* a little backward, if not totally out of it. If the Yankees sweep Milwaukee in the next three games . . . Now that's something I can get into.

"What if we went with just a yaw . . . ?" Stop the world—it's pitching too badly—I want to get off!

4:11 p.m.: Back on the bridge. Before we start shooting this scene Mr. Wise does a pick-up of . . . guess what? A closeup of Mr. Chekov when the Captain first comes aboard the ship. It's been six weeks since I had the temerity to question his coverage of my character and so thoroughly embarrassed myself. It's also six weeks since I misjudged the man's steel-trap mind and his overall concept of the characters we play. If it's possible, I'm even more embarrassed now.

5:17 p.m.: The scene we discussed at the rehearsal table is now being practiced on the bridge. In addition to yaws and pitches, it involves our first close encounter with the formidable enemy that makes up the bulk of the movie's plot. It's another overlapping scene where the speeches tumble out one after the other from Kirk, Decker, Spock, Sulu, Uhura, the Gravity Control Technician, the Damage Repair Technician, the Environmental Engineering Technician, the Engineering Technician (the two Ralphs, Iva, and Franklyn), and Chekov.

As the sequence progresses several light changes are called for. The alien's weapon (a form of plasma energy) hits our deflector screens with whiplash energy bolts. As a result, we go from standard bridge light to darkness to auxiliary life-support systems to an eerie green light as the energy bolt fills our viewer screen and bathes the bridge. It is the perfect example of organized chaos and we are required to rehearse it a dozen times. When you see it on the screen it will appear smoothly structured and fluid, but we haven't achieved that yet. In addition to our director's own sense of professional integrity, there is the company feeling of responsibility to the fans to be better than any other science-fiction movie and better than we were as a television series. It's not something we generally discuss, but it is something we all feel, and whether we succeed or not, it won't be for lack of trying. And so we rehearse some more.

7:10 p.m.: Our longest day and the shot is still not in the can, but we'll get it tomorrow.

TUESDAY, SEPTEMBER 19

Yesterday in rehearsal, today on celluloid; a bolt of green whiplash energy scores a hit against our deflector screens—from several different angles.

11:15 a.m.: After waiting two hours for new dimmers to complete the bridge light changes and new 8-mm tapes for the science console (new dangers necessitate new read-outs on the panels), we get the shot rehearsed so long yesterday afternoon. Oh, yes, yaw and pitch are 60 degrees and 40 degrees, respectively. Exactly as they were originally written.

11:30 a.m.: Gene comes by and tells me he has read the Buck Rogers Big Little Book I gave him for his birthday. He is so pleased I am wondering if it might not be too late to suggest we find a place for Killer Kane among our antagonists.

12:30 p.m.: Lunch. George has come away from home without his wallet. He requests a loan. I'm rich; I have five dollars. We order tuna salads at the refurbished Paramount cafeteria and discover too late that my sawbuck won't carry us through. The cashier is looking for a guard as one of the maintenance men behind us in line voluntarily dips into a ragged pocket and withdraws the red-inked seventy cents. These *Star Trek* actors are really high rollers!

There is a curious and ironic contradiction in the socio-political posture of the film industry. Today's motion pictures frequently make statements promoting human dignity and human rights and are sincerely motivated when they do so. But no matter how conscientious the effort in front of the camera, behind it exists the last bastion of feudalism. Nowhere is the caste system more glorified than there, and that means *every* motion picture and television soundstage in Hollywood. This caste system comes in two packages, professional and psychological.

The first one is so rigid that if you know the code you can determine the tenant for each rung by the number of steps he has to walk from his car to the soundstage. Basically, there are four classes of performers: the Extras, the Bit Players (God, what a term!), the "Supporting Actors," and the Stars. The Extras, in the professional order of things, occupy the lowest station. They are the "atmosphere," the people who by the simple presence of their bodies establish the atmosphere of the scene. They are considered nonpeople, walking costumes, the background colors. Stand-ins are also Extras but are deemed more important because they generally stay with a series or movie for its entirety. They do so because it is their job to stand in for the supporting actors and stars when the composition of a scene is first being designed by the lighting and camera people. On a television series, in particular, they have added respectability because they frequently perform small favors for the show leads and consequently, to a degree, have the weight of that power source behind them.

The second category in the class hierarchy contains those actors with very small parts. Generally, they come in for a day or, in the case of our additional bridge personnel, they are around a lot but have very little to do. I've never been sure whether "bit" player refers to the itty-bitty parts they play or to the tacit understanding that they are only a bit of a player—not yet a whole person. Frequently, bit players remain bit players all their lives and are so catalogued on casting lists. (In the case of our group they are all young, just starting out, and extremely talented. I would suspect that in time they will all rise above that appellation.)

The supporting actors come in various forms and are generally those with the "featured" or "co-star" billing in the project. Jimmy, George, Nichelle, and I are the "various forms" in our picture.

The fourth group is the nose-bleed niche—the stars. In the *Star Trek* movie it is, of course, the province of our holy triumvirate and Steve and Persis.

The point in detailing these groupings here is that along with the obvious disparity in monetary reward, there are a dozen more subtle ways by which each is distinguished from the other. For example, as a general rule in the production of Hollywood films, extras must find their own parking outside the studios on whatever street it is available. Often space will be provided for bit players in parking lots beyond the studio walls. The supporting actors get to park within the gates but frequently up to several blocks away from where they are working. The stars step out of their Jags and through the heavy steel doors of the soundstage.

The stars are given personalized "director" chairs to rest their weary bottoms. Sometimes the supporting actors are also so indulged. The buns of the bit players (sounds like the title of a foreign movie) must scavenge for a seat among whatever few non-claimed chairs may be available. The extras are usually relegated to benches in a dark corner.

If a scene calls for all orders to participate, then the highest ones will be called last in the morning and, to further accommodate them, will be excused first.

A reasonable case can be made for this prejudicial conduct on the basis that it is the stars who sell the product, and then to a lesser degree and in descending order the others. It is not, however, the attitude of management that I find so oppressive, but how these groups relate to each other, their personal interactions, the psychological aspect of the caste system that I referred to earlier.

The unwritten law seems to say that not only as performers but as *people* the extras are the least meritorious and the stars the most. There are people within these groups who frown upon this stratification, but they do it pretty much into their shirtfronts. Nobody says much about it, nobody *does* anything about it. And yet I know that everybody is aware of it. It makes me wonder just how much of the cordiality between these groups then is just sublimated hostility directed upward by those on the bottom and sanctimonious noblesse oblige directed downward by those on top. What a waste of human dignity. Workers of the world, unite. You've got nothing to lose but your false sense of self!

4:05 p.m.: It begins to look now as if I won't be working today. They've been shooting "the attack" from angles that don't incorporate my console. I retire to my dressing room and am met by three young women who have managed to gain access to the lot by presenting themselves as prospective employees wishing to fill out job applications. Like many fans around the country, they would like to stage a Star Trek convention. Conventions have long ago ceased to exist as a means to bringing the show back. They have become an end unto themselves. A living entity that functions independent of a cause. A place to convene and commune and maybe even cohabitate. A microcosmic society, an oasis, if you will, in the heart of the real world where everyone shares the same interest, acts with tolerance toward each other, puts aside the pressures of getting by "out there" and abandons himself to fantasy and the child within him. Not a bad place, at that.

The three young women and I do a lot of speculating on what effect, if any, *Star Trek—The Motion Picture* will have on conventions, our own lives, and people in general. We take turns championing the cause and playing devil's advocate.

We say good-bye to each other, having resolved nothing. And, of course, isn't that the way it should be? George and I decided way back in August that this film project and what came after would be grand adventure for us.

"Follow the yellow brick road, Dorothy."

WEDNESDAY, SEPTEMBER 20

Can a man take fire in his bosom and his clothes not be burned?

Proverbs 6:27

In my case, it's the other way around—hopefully—because today Chekov is supposed to go up in flames.

7:30 a.m.: My earliest set call, but, the hour notwith-standing, I'm all revved up and hot to get burned, as the saying goes. Actually, the effect finally decided on will be a combination of flashing green lights, post-production animation, and a smoke-enveloped limb courtesy of the interaction of acetic acid and ammonia. The live fire idea has finally been rejected as too mun-dane. It has been decided that the whiplash energy bolt causing Pavel's peril is too sophisticated and too ad-vanced to be classified in the same league with your everyday Bunsen burner. And here I thought that the decision to not torch my back was based on humani-tarian considerations.

7:44 a.m.: Since my sleeve gets scorched, it stands to reason that the arm under it suffers a similar fate. Fred tells me, therefore, that he will have to shave both my hand (alas, I'm one of those throwbacks with hair on my knuckles) and my forearm to prevent the vinyl "blisters" he will eventually apply from painfully dep-ilating my skin when removed.

Even though only the right hand and arm are to be burned, he proceeds to shave the left ones as well. The logic is faultless: the two limbs have to match. This is not, after all, a scene from *Let That Be Your Last Battlefield*. These aren't aliens we're talking about here in a trifling four-hundred-thousand-dollar television episode. This is Lieutenant Pavel Chekov, the *Enter-prise*'s finest Russian lieutenant, performing in a twenty-four-million-dollar motion picture. Respect must be shown. Care must be taken. Everything must be per-fect.

It is only after the shearing has been completed and I hold up my limbs, now pale, waxy and resembling nothing so much as the underbelly of dead fish, that it occurs to me that although my members now match each other, they do not match any shot of the weaponry officer's arms that has so far been made!

9:33 a.m.: I have often been asked what basically is the difference between stage acting and film acting. There are the obvious differences in vocal projection and audience contact, but the scene I've just completed is a good example of the less apparent but more fundamental distinction in the two forms of the craft as defined here.

A stage play permits sustained involvement by the actor and gives him considerable emotional and physical freedom. In effect, it allows him to be as good as he can be and, therefore, leaves him open to a fair assessment of his talent. The stage performance, then, is the conclusive test of thespian ability.

A film performance is accomplished in short bursts, sometimes as brief as a few seconds, rarely longer than two or three minutes. Also, in this medium there is the opportunity to retake a scene many times to achieve the desired result. The audience, viewing only the finished edited product and not the framework in which it is accomplished, can be misguided therefore into believing that they have been witness to talent greater than that which actually exists.

The other side of the coin, however, is that the restraints imposed by limited camera mobility and accompanying light and sound restrictions demand a craftsmanship in the celluloid performance that is different and sometimes more difficult than in "live" acting.

In my small scene, for example, I had to "feel" the energy bolt travel through my hand and up my arm. As that happens I am to spin around in my chair and swing my hand past my body and above it. I must then hold it there for several beats so that the animation burn that envelops my arm (achieved later in the lab) will be clearly visible. At the same time my face must be positioned so as to catch the light from the "Baby Junior" over my shoulder. When I rise from my chair I must be sure to come up slowly enough so that the camera can keep me in frame while it pans up with me. I am then to toe the marks placed on the floor in front of me lest I step too far forward and beyond the focus point of the lens.

Nothing to it, you say, and you would not be wrong if it weren't also true that all the time I am executing the choreography I am also supposed to believe that the energy bolt is executing me and react accordingly. Since the camera is close enough to expose the holes in my teeth, it is also close enough to expose the holes in my performance, should my anguish not be totally credible. And even though my oratory through all this is a consonant short of a single word (all I get to do is scream "AAAARRRRRGGGGGHHHHHH!"), there is still considerable technique involved in fulfilling the demands both physical and visceral in this small piece of acting.

Because the performance situation described here is not unique, but, on the contrary, commonplace in the business of cinematic histrionics, it is all the more illustrative of the problems in this medium that the actor must endure and overcome.

Most simply stated, then, the camera performer's responsibility is to first satisfy the machinery, then himself, and then his audience. The noble grimacier who troddeth the boards does, to a much greater degree, worry only about the latter two.

11:31 a.m.: The zap shot is in the can and now I retire to the makeup room for the first-stage burn application. Charlie Schram, our new makeup man in charge of first-, second-, and third-degree burns, tries "Pink Cafe" lipstick for the intial skin reaction but the color washes out under the green lights. He then goes to "Sensual Red," a shade out of Sadie Thompson, and we record another shot for posterity.

For the second stage and the next take he adds bottled ashes (whose, I'm wondering).

The vinyl blisters are next applied, and now the special effects people move in, too. Alex wraps my bare arm in aluminum foil, covers that with a heavy pad, and then pulls the sleeve of my shirt down over both.

Just before the camera rolls he dabs the area with the solutions of ammonia and acetic acid, which, in interaction, create the smoke effect that makes Chekov appear to be in deep trouble. Never mind, Chekov, *Koenig* is in deep trouble. The solutions have seeped through at the edge of the aluminum foil and are making contact with my skin. To hell with it, the show must go on, and—who knows?—maybe it will make Chekov's reaction more believable. Anything for a better performance.

4:08 p.m.: Is my dedication rewarded? Is my martyrdom applauded? The last shot of the sequence has me being helped toward sickbay. Before we start rehearsing it, Mr. Wise suggests that I pull up my sagging pants. Mr. Shatner rejoins that better I should pull down my legs. Cute, Bill, cute. Amidst the gales of laughter that sweep the bridge, I am wondering how Larry Olivier would have handled this.

7:00 p.m.: I return to the warmth of hearth and home. Here, at least, I am loved. But, alas, I am not the man I had once been. Judy looks at my pale hairless arms and declares that she is put in mind of a matched set of albino woodchucks. Josh insists that I look like a gorilla trying on a human costume. Danielle exclaims, "Gross!" and flees the room. "Oh, that this too, too solid flesh would melt . . ."

THURSDAY, SEPTEMBER 21

Wherein the entity breaks off its attack to the surprise of everyone but Chekov. Which isn't much of a surprise since Chekov has been carted off to sickbay and isn't there to see it.

I'm not scheduled for today and perhaps for several days thereafter because the ensuing action covers six and one-half pages and we have recently been averaging two and one-half pages a day. When we were doing the series we completed an entire sixty-five-page episode in six days. At the rate we are going now, it would have taken us well over a month for each show. Robert Wise shoots his films with great care, and, of course, the special effects have slowed us up considerably, but motion pictures in general have a far longer shooting schedule than do TV shows.

Obviously, if you have to get an episode out every week, you have to work faster. Unfortunately, along with the dizzy pace there is a concomitant sacrifice in quality. It is not happenstance that the "Star Trek" programs acknowledged to be least successful were those filmed during our third year when the network's edict that the shows be brought in on time included the tacit understanding that it be accomplished at all costs.

It is, in fact, rather extraordinary that we were able

to hit on so many cylinders so consistently. I remember, for example, that during the filming of "The Way to Eden" the director became so burdened by the pressure to complete shooting on schedule that he insisted I block my own scene for the camera while he was off preparing another setup. I won't take the responsibility for the spottiness of that episode, but my experience does point up the problems inherent in forcing the pace to meet television deadlines. So far, at least, Paramount has had the eminently good sense not to try to rush this production.

FRIDAY, SEPTEMBER 22

Today the decision is made to bring the Enterprise within the boundary of the energy-field cloud and toward its command nucleus. Our mission is to stop this thing from destroying Earth. We have no choice but to push forward.

2:00 p.m.: Set call. Chekov is still absent from the sequence but Director Wise wants to momentarily backtrack for another setup of Wednesday's suffering, and so I have been called back in.

For the purpose of a later story point, Lieutenant Ilia and Dr. Chapel have to establish a rapport with each other. It is achieved here when Ilia administers a "Deltan touch" to Chekov while Dr. Chapel watches. A look between them and flickering smiles are sufficient to accomplish the task.

Once that is out of the way, the good doctor produces an impressive-looking piece of "medical equipment" with which she sprays "plasti-skin" on the wounded Russian's ailing parts. I have no idea what the concoction is that she bathes me with, but now in addition to the effects of lipstick, ashes, and vinyl blisters, my skin also feels slippery and slimy. It's a good thing I love show business.

3:45 p.m.: The shot is in the can. While waiting to be released, I talk at length with Persis for the first time. She possesses a most interesting combination of seemingly contradictory personality traits. By turns, she is the poised elegant international model, a guileless young girl who takes ingenious delight in her own beauty and an actor like the rest of us fraught with self-doubt and insecurity. On the screen the diverse elements come together in a delicate balance of sophistication and vulnerability. The effect is a charisma that has little to do with talent but which, embodied in the right role, can make a performer a star. I am betting that the part of Lieutenant Ilia will do that for Persis.

4:50 p.m.: I receive my call sheet for Monday. I have to be in at 1:30. I'll be needed then for Chekov's post-sickbay return to the bridge.

Somehow I thought it would take longer to shoot the sequences preceding it. I am only too painfully aware, after all, that a full six and one-half pages are played out on the screen while the roasted Russian is missing from his post. Are we then picking up the pace, shooting more pages per day? Shall we finish filming the script earlier? Shall Koenig be excused from this production sooner than anticipated? Shall the fun go from his life? Shall his pockets grow lighter while his lightheartedness grows heavier? Shall there be no God in Heaven, Yankees in the World Series, and little old ladies in Leningrad? Tune in Monday.

MONDAY, SEPTEMBER 25

The crew reacts as the Enterprise *passes deeper and deeper into the cloud. The effects incorporated here if rendered as conceived will be truly extraordinary—not something simply bigger and better than has gone before in science-fiction movies, but a whole new frame of reference. A new plane, a new dimension, a whole new experience for us all.*

8:35 a.m.: "Walter, this is Kevin. Could you come in immediately?" So much for my 1:30 call.

9:45 a.m.: On the set and in makeup. I'm getting smarter now. I do not change into my uniform until I am specifically told to do so. For one thing, I have learned that if my call is later than 8:30 the chances are I won't work before lunch. For another thing, getting in and out of my uniform has become a trial in my life. Since I started getting burned, I've been wearing the very tight-fitting Reuben shirt. It has no zippers and fits so snugly that it literally takes two people to get it over one overdeveloped head. Michael Lynn is one of the costumers who helps me into this thing. The procedure he employs is a bit unnerving. He completely wraps my face in a silk scarf as he closes the door to my dressing room. (I always couple these two actions because silk scarf-wrapped heads seem decadent, if not downright kinky, and should only be effected behind closed doors. I mean, if the first sentence of a story read, "He closed the door to his room as he wrapped his face in a silk scarf," wouldn't you think you had opened a dirty book?) The scarf is used to prevent my makeup from rubbing off on the neckline of my uniform. The silk material is not porous and after thirty seconds I am convinced I am suffocating. (I can see the headline: "SEMI-NUDE ACTOR STRANGLES IN SILK SCARF BEHIND CLOSED DOORS.") The procedure takes more than thirty seconds because the opening in the shirt is so narrow and my dome so large. In fact, with each succeeding unsuccessful pass I am convinced that my head is growing in size and so am left with the prospect of either suffocating or becoming a hydrocephalic. Either way, my view of things remains as dim as my view of things inside the scarf and brightens on both counts only when the bloody thing is finally removed.

11:18 a.m.: On the soundstage. Leonard sits down in a nearby chair. It occurs to me while we are talking that I have never spoken to him at sufficient length to determine whether the somewhat taciturn and sober presentation he makes is nine parts Spock or nine parts Nimoy. I am only sure that the character he plays is a wonder to behold. I find myself as Chekov being comforted by his presence. It is a mark of Leonard's command of his portrayal that when I step onto the set and assume the Russian identity I have immediate well-defined feelings about the Vulcan across from me. How bad can wormholes and whiplash energy bolts be when they don't seem to ruffle our science officer? I have concluded, therefore, that when I take that airplane flight where the motors fall off and we drop like a bucket from the sky, I want Spock beside me saying, "Interesting." Whether I'd settle for Leonard Nimoy in those circumstances is the point of my original question, *vis-à-vis* to what degree are the actor and the character he plays the same person.

I know that Leonard has written a book with a

title that apparently defines his feelings on the matter, but I also know that when we perform roles truthfully (and there isn't a false note in the character of the Vulcan), we draw upon ourselves for the source material. The person we play may not be the face we show the world out of makeup, but, nonetheless, the germ of that being is tucked away inside us somewhere waiting to be liberated, waiting for license (the script and the camera) to develop and give itself expression.

I guess, then, that even without any telling statement from him in our conversation, I have answered my own question. Even if the qualities of the Vulcan are not operational in Leonard's everyday life, they are an organic part of him. Spock-Nimoy are a compound, not a mixture, and cannot be separated.

What I do learn about in our talk is the one-man show on the life of Van Gogh with which he has begun to tour the country. He is able to report that the audiences have been very responsive. Despite the fact that both the artist and the Vulcan are known (among other things) for ear anomalies, they are as disparate as two characters could be. Leonard's success in the part is obviously testimony to his multi-dimensional personality and a tribute to his versatility as a performer.

What impresses me most, however, is that he not only performs the part, but that he has written much of the script as well. It sounds to me like the perfect marriage for expression in two art forms.

It sets my imagination to racing. Maybe I should put something together based on the life of *Anton* Chekov . . . or maybe Fyodor Dostoevsky. . . . Would you believe Nikita Khrushchev . . . Akim Tamiroff? The last idea isn't so farfetched. My father and Akim were buddies together in Chicago during the late Twenties. When I was ten we visited California and the movie set on which the Russian actor was working. We were introduced and he looked down at me all bushy-browed, heavy-jowled, and bulbous-nosed, and said, "You loook juz lahk me ven I wuz liddel boy!" Something to look forward to.

11:39 a.m.: Persis is concerned about the nude scene written into the script for her. She hasn't been able to get assurances from the front office that she will be wearing a body stocking. I'm concerned, too. Chekov is supposed to see her in this condition. Dirty old man!

12:30 p.m.: Smart move not getting into my costume. This way I don't have to get out of it now. Every lunch hour all costumes are cleaned up and pressed for the afternoon's work.

2:11 p.m.: I've just learned that the script currently runs two hours and forty-three minutes. Since Paramount is reluctant to release the film at longer than two hours and ten minutes, the third act rewrites now in progress are for cutting as well as content.

Maybe that's why I haven't yet reappeared on the bridge today as promised. My mind immediately flashes on the dialogue to explain it:

MCCOY: Chekov's burns were worse than we thought.
KIRK: Yes?
MCCOY: He's dead, Jim.

5:10 p.m.: I am released from the soundstage, discharged from sickbay but not fired from the production. My reappearance on the bridge will be shot on Wednesday (tomorrow they're back in engineering). Just like General MacArthur, I shall return!

WEDNESDAY, SEPTEMBER 27

Today the crew gets to see what's at the center-heart-liver of the cloud. Again, I've got my fingers crossed that the optical effects people will bring this off. You'll get your money's worth right here if they do.

8:00 a.m.: First order of business is to reshave my hands. I'm wearing a new long-sleeved Reuben shirt, so my arms needn't be worked on, too. (For some reason, they haven't dressed me in the sickbay outfit designed for my return to the bridge.)

The next order of business is the plasti-skin application. The stuff they are using is a plastic sealer that isn't made anymore and has been sitting in a jug for twenty years. It dries with a gloss and gives the appearance of a fabricated shiny new skin. Although purportedly the same, this is an entirely different goop than that which spurted from Dr. Chapel's pressurized "medical instrument." This concoction is too thick and oozy to function as a spray. The other stuff, I now discover, was salad oil. I am beginning to wonder if my hand, like in that old movie *The Beast with Five Fingers,* might not crawl up my chest and choke me while I sleep in retribution for putting it through such indignities.

11:25 a.m.: The sequence now being shot is the one where Chekov, fresh from sickbay, emerges from the elevator onto the bridge in the company of Dr. McCoy. It is done in two setups: a master shot with a 50-mm lens that encompasses Sulu, Ilia, Spock, Decker, Uhura, and the two of us; and then in a closeup with a 75-mm lens of just De and me. The action at the moment is the reactions of McCoy and Chekov to seeing the

CHEKOV'S ENTERPRISE

A nice Russian lieutenant minding his own business.

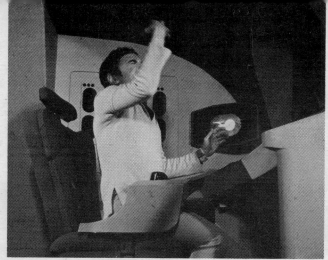

There are obviously no rewards for niceness.

Whiplashed by a green energy bolt.

". . . 'tis not so deep as a well, nor wide as a church door . . ."

The Deltan Touch—better than novocaine.

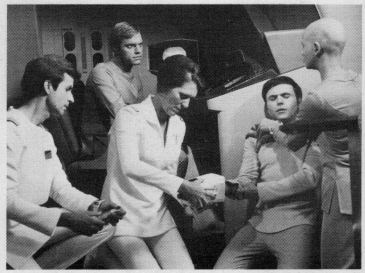

Dr. Chapel and her traveling plasti-skin applicator—better than Palmolive.

This either is the look of intense concentration or the pitcher has just bitten his tongue.

Note the stunning form. Note the stunning legs. Note the stunned look on Steve Collins's face as the ball sails over the left field fence for a home run.

The *Star Trek* softball team. Note who among the cast has a terrific sense of camera presence.

New York Star Trek Convention. Question from the audience: "What was it like working with the cast again after so many years?" Answer: "Read *Chekov's Enterprise*, that fast reading, entertaining, informative . . ."

Take-out lunch for one hundred hosted by George, Nichelle and Walter. Note that George, Nichelle and Walter aren't going near the food.

Party celebrating Persis's and Steve's birthdays and Bill's having found a place to rest his arm. Note Mr. Spock's look of uncontrollable euphoria.

This is Chekov's being-sucked-into-the-wormhole grimace.
Note how Decker refuses to look at Chekov during these
histrionics.

It's either a present from an Australian fan handmade from hundreds of daisies or the shirt emblem for a new alien crew member.

Watching cataclysmic events on the Rec Deck view screen. Among the crew are one hundred fifty of *Star Trek*'s most devoted fans. Note the one with the autograph book.

Kirk, inside V'ger, looks to be in trouble. Inside the *Enterprise* a troubled Sulu and Uhura look to Chekov for a decision. Chekov looks inside his head for the solution and concludes they're *all* in trouble.

Targeting the asteroid on Chekov's weaponry console. Note the subtle highlighting and shading on Decker's and Chekov's faces.

Kirk is "out there" in grave jeopardy. A moment of intense concern for those aboard. Note which crew member has already read the end of the script.

The day after Thanksgiving. The last bridge scene is finally completed. A time for rejoicing. Note Mr. Spock's look of uncontrollable euphoria.

entity up close for the first time. De has the words and delivers them with just the right touch of humor to counterpoint a situation fraught with danger.

Whatever comedic lines the script possesses are the unchallenged province of Dr. McCoy. I can think of no one better qualified to carry off the wryness demanded than De Forest. I also can think of no one (other than myself) I'd be happier to see get the opportunity.

De is one of the genuinely nice people in the business. He is one actor who seems incapable of pretense and sham. I have always found him very straightforward and honest. There are people who abuse these qualities by using candor as an excuse for crudity, but not so with "Bones's" alter ego. I've never seen him lack sensitivity in dealings with his fellow man. You can tell I'm very pleased to consider him a friend.

3:44 p.m.: It does not look as if I'll be working anymore this afternoon. In progress now is "single" coverage of everyone who was in the master shot as they reacted to seeing the object in the center of the energy-field cloud. Since practically the entire complement with the exception of De and myself were included in that tableau, it seems a safe bet that the rest of the day will be devoted to these individual setups.

Danny McCauley, the first assistant director, is reluctant, however, to approach Robert Wise about releasing people early. It is possible that the current camera angle can be used for another scene somewhere else in the story, and our director might decide on a moment's notice to shoot that sequence while the lights are in the proper position. There is the added possibility that we'll finish all the scheduled stuff quicker than anticipated and start new work for which an excused actor might otherwise have been needed. The chances of these things happening are minimal but not without precedent, and so I remain available and uncomplaining. "Those also serve who stand and wait"—I keep telling myself.

Mel Traxel is our still photographer. He is with us all day every day. Looking at him, I am put in mind of those pictures of Mexican soldiers with munitions belts crisscrossing their chests. In Mel's case it's a host of camera straps that hang across his body as he clicks —clicks—clicks the same action that the motion picture camera is recording. He tells me that he shoots about eight rolls of film a day. On our approximately one-hundred-day shooting schedule, that comes out to about 64,000 exposures! I can't imagine how he manages to choose the ones that will eventually be used for the intended publicity purposes.

5:29 p.m.: In our story the adversary sends out a probe that invades our ship. The last shot of the day is a test of a special effect designed by Abel and Associates to achieve this illusion. If it looks okay in tomorrow morning's dailies, we will proceed to shoot the sequence in which it comes aboard. Since actors are not required for the test, we are all now released.

On the way out I am told my set call for tomorrow is 9:00. If my formula is correct, it means I will not work before lunch. Let's see, how does that go again? "Those also serve who . . ."

THURSDAY, SEPTEMBER 28

Yesterday wormholes, today plasma energy probes. Nobody said being an officer on the U.S.S. Enterprise would be easy.

11:00 a.m.: We haven't begun the probe episode yet and the delays seem without end. At one point I am told that when the blue screen is changed to a black screen we will begin. I don't know why that exchange must be made, but I do know it's been an hour since it was done and we still haven't dusted off our duffs.

By now every copy of the *L.A. Times* crossword puzzle has been filled in. Even the generally stolid and reclusive Mr. Nimoy is showing signs of ennui. He is out on the soundstage engaged in a hotly contested game of backgammon. I find myself curiously affected on two counts by Leonard's animated participation.

First, I find it reassuring to see him absorbed in this mundane competition with Brenda Gooch, one of the stand-ins on the production and acknowledged backgammon expert. It is as if by doing so he is bridging the gap between his status and the rest of the work complement on our project. Breaking down the old caste lines, so to speak.

The second aspect of my response is more cerebral than emotional. I have already suggested that with stardom goes privilege. With privilege goes a sense of self-importance which, because it is a condition applicable to all mankind, is less a symptom of human frailty than it is of human nature. It is difficult to believe, therefore, that Leonard, sitting here and playing the game with a large circle of people watching, does not now feel in some recess of his mind that in doing so "he has walked among us."

How can I be making this critical assessment of his motivation when at the same time I feel good about his presence here? It is a worrisome ambiguity that I am trying to sort out in my mind. The conclusion I am approaching is that my original tract on the self-imposed psychological stratification of performers needs some amending. Perhaps it was naïve of me to assume that the pigeonholing we do even in regard to ourselves is open to conscious manipulation. The noblesse oblige directed downward and the hostility directed upward are consequences of the system and cannot be changed just by willing it. So long as we have stars and "others," we will have castes. It is society and not the individual who does the cataloguing.

Of course, I have never suggested that I am an objective noneditorial observer of my fellow man (captive as I am to a somewhat skewed, if not downright pathological, perspective of life), and I wouldn't be a bit surprised if the erudite barber's son before me thought my interpretation of his activity totally whacko.

While I am confessing my neurotic bent, I should admit, too, that whenever I see Leonard and Bill in *sotto voce* conversation, I suspect that if they're not actually discussing their most recent top-secret conversation with the President of the United States, then at least they are exchanging views on their most recent top-secret conversation with the president of Paramount.

11:45 a.m.: We are released early for lunch. The probe test made yesterday afternoon is now back from the lab, and Abel, Wise, and Roddenberry (sounds like either the perfect double-play combination or a great vaudeville act) are anxious to screen it.

A collection was taken up earlier this morning for a take-out Chinese lunch, and eleven of us now repair to Stage Ten for the feast. In our group are Michael, Danny, Ronnie and Liz (wardrobe), Ve and Janna (makeup), Barbara (hairdresser), Pat (seamstress), and George, Leonard, and me. The conversation around the table involves the sexual consequences of yeast infections.

3:20 p.m.: The effects test must have been all right because we are now ready to rehearse the sequence introducing the probe.

The probe phenomenon as devised by Abel will be mounted in two stages. The second part will be created in the lab and will be animated snake-like tendrils of energy that whiplash around the bridge, running our consoles, acquiring information, and in general causing havoc. These plasma energy tendrils will be animated into the action recorded live on the set. That action is the first stage of the effect, and the source of the tendrils, the probe itself.

It stands before us now: an eight-foot-high, sixty-pound lavender cylinder filled (in a partial vacuum) with zeon gas. When the probe is "on," the gas is ignited through a trailing cable by 90,000 volts of electricity. The partial vacuum (same principle as a light bulb) is employed to create an intense strobe light without burning oxygen and creating a heat situation that might lead to an explosion. (We certainly don't want an explosion, do we?)

I could swear that the light is brighter than the F-11 (daylight) photostop I am told it is, but then the bridge is quite dark at this point. In addition, the probe strobe (there's definitely a song title here) is pulsating at twenty-four beats per second, and that may be another reason for my sensory bank overload.

When the camera rolls, a goggle-protected employee of Abel dressed in white and looking not unlike a *Star Wars* storm trooper grasps the cylinder by handles placed near the top and bottom. Lifting the apparatus the way one would a mattress through a narrow doorway, he rotates it in small circles.

Although the camera is shooting past us and directly at the zeon cylinder, the man holding it is not visible because the brilliance of the light washes out his white suit.

4:17 p.m.: Our action during this first setup is basically to attempt to keep the ship functioning while shielding our eyes from the probe. The action behind the camera during this first setup is basically to attempt to get the shot. Never before have we gone so long in a day without at least one take in the can. I keep thinking of the time and money being spent. If these expenditures equate well with the results, the *Star Trek* motion picture will be the visual experience of the decade. I console myself with that prospect.

As with all the 65-mm footage, the camera and its personnel belong to Abel. The Paramount crew can do nothing but wait until the highly technical effect is achieved. The actors can do nothing but wait until the highly technical effect is achieved and wonder if in the process our corneas aren't being burned out.

5:05 p.m.: I am determined to get an expression of feeling from Leonard regarding his participation in this film. I ask him if he is having fun and, hesitating not a whit, he says, "Yes." Subsequently, there are qualifications, but as I start for home this evening it is with the sure knowledge that his fondness for Spock, for Star Trek, for his co-workers has not abated during the intervening years. Once and for all that should put to rest the virulent and pervasive rumor of his discontent.

FRIDAY, SEPTEMBER 29

The probe is still probing the Enterprise. *We're still probing to find the way to help it do it right.*

11:15 a.m.: Today's shoot is starting as slowly as the preceding one. Suspecting as much, I suggest to Janna Phillips (now in charge of my makeup) that she resist the impulse to swab my hand in twenty-year sealer until we are sure I will be called to the set. I am still waiting.

The shot they are trying for this morning is the reverse of yesterday's. The cylinder is now stationed in the foreground and the camera shoots past it toward the crew. Since it is one of our standard master setups, my console isn't visible and hence I am not needed.

On this day the Abel man manipulating the huge canister is dressed totally in black (looking more like Darth Vader now). It turns out that the white suit used Thursday was visible on the film, after all.

12:00 p.m.: My brother, Norm, visits for the first time. Like everyone else who has come by, he is thoroughly captivated by the magnificent sets. I direct him to a position on the bridge from which he can watch the action and still be safely beyond the camera lens.

4:05 p.m.: Neither Nichelle nor I has yet worked. Her desire to participate is as strong as mine, and a raging boredom has set in for both of us. Fortunately, we also share a somewhat warped sense of humor, a condition we have on more than one occasion taken advantage of to relieve our frustrations. Little do we know that this is one such occasion.

John Dresden, an actor playing a security guard, comes over and the three of us sit together on the dark soundstage trying to keep each other awake. Idle minds, alas, are the devil's playmates, for now one of the secretaries (she shall remain nameless) enters the soundstage and innocently asks about the day's activities. What follows is really only supposed to be a thirty-second put-on, but it rapidly outgrows its proscenium and becomes in short order a full-fledged production of the theater of the absurd:

SECRETARY: What's happening?

WALTER: You mean since the fight between Bill and Leonard?

SECRETARY [rocked]: What fight?

NICHELLE: Isn't that why you're here?

SECRETARY: I haven't heard a thing about it!

WALTER: Leonard slugged Bill.

SECRETARY [shocked]: You're kidding?!

NICHELLE: It was horrible.

SECRETARY: But why?

WALTER: I don't think it's for us to say.

NICHELLE: Of course what Bill then did to Leonard . . .

WALTER: Pulled his ears off.

SECRETARY [stupefied]: My God!

WALTER [turning to John]: Tell her the rest.

JOHN: It happened so fast. I was just trying to get out of the way.

SECRETARY: What did Robert Wise do?

WALTER: Told them to settle their differences with a game of cards. Was it Hearts or Canasta?

NICHELLE: Didn't make any difference, because then Bill picked up and went home. Said he wasn't coming back ever.

SECRETARY [rocked, shocked, and stupefied]: MY GOD! ! !

WALTER: And now they're going to have to bring up some portable units and shoot Bill's scenes at his house.

NICHELLE: Shatner said that from now on he was going to phone in his performances.

WALTER: And, of course, that upset Nichelle because she doesn't have all that much to do *now* as Com-

munications Officer, and if Bill starts doing his own
phoning . . .

[Enter Leonard. He has absolutely no idea about what
is going on as he sits down in his chair.]

NICHELLE: How are you feeling, Leonard?

LEONARD: Okay.

NICHELLE: I mean since the fight.

LEONARD: The fight?

NICHELLE: With Bill.

LEONARD [as it dawns]: Oh.

SECRETARY: What happened?

LEONARD: I'd rather not talk about it.

[The secretary now takes Leonard's hand sympatheti-
cally. He doesn't resist.]

SECRETARY: Does Gene know about this?

LEONARD [firmly]: I'd rather not talk about it.

[At this point Bill crosses past us, looking, as if on cue,
very upset. I discover later that his car has sprung a
leak.]

NICHELLE: Well, well, well. So he came back.

LEONARD: That's always been a characteristic of his.

WALTER [accusingly]: Let me tell you something,
Leonard. In this case I happen to think Bill was
absolutely right.

LEONARD: He has often been in the past.

NICHELLE [with rising anger toward me]: How can you
say that?!

WALTER [starting to shout]: I have a right to my
opinion!

LEONARD [in full throat]: Hey, now hold it a minute!

WALTER [starting to leave]: I've had enough of this.

NICHELLE: You come back here, damn it!!

WALTER: Like hell I will!

At which point I leave the soundstage. I don't know
what transpires after that, but when I return a few min-

utes later the secretary is still trying to console Leonard, who is bravely suffering in silence. I finally go up to her and explain that we were only joking, but she won't believe it. She insists we are just trying to cover up the fight between the two stars. It is only after repeated assurances that she finally accepts my story. Frankly, she looks a bit disappointed. I guess it's a slow day on her job, too.

October

SUNDAY, OCTOBER 1

11:00 a.m.: The first practice of the *Star Trek* softball team is underway. Among the actors who show up are Bill, Steve, George, and myself. Jim Chirco, the craft serviceman who dispenses the dried chicken soup, among other duties, has organized a league of Paramount shows for the benefit of the Muscular Dystrophy Association. Presumably, in subsequent weeks we will play "Happy Days," "Laverne and Shirley," "Taxi," and "Little House on the Prairie."

If today's practice is any indication of what's in store, we'd be better off matching up with the Bad News Bears.

MONDAY, OCTOBER 2

Today a security guard (who else?) and seven pages get zapped. A piqued probe is responsible for the security guard. A piqued Paramount is responsible for our shortened story. We're still under orders to bring the picture in at two hours and ten minutes.

10:00 a.m.: The day isn't starting out too good. For one thing, I've absolutely blown my set call. Having read the wrong column on the call sheet, I show up at 9:30 for makeup instead of 8:45. For another, the Yankees lost yesterday on the last day of the season and have to play the Red Sox *in Boston* today in a one-game playoff.

I am already wondering if my tardiness is a bad omen: Will the Yankees be tardy in scoring runs? Don't laugh. When you're a superstitious baseball fan *and* a S.T. actor, you are permitted certain irrational excesses on the day of the big game. I won't go so far as to say I'd throw a salt monster over my shoulder if a Horta crossed my path (I told you the day wasn't starting out too good), but then you can be sure I won't be walking under any anti-gravitational ladders, either.

2:00 p.m.: I have my portable TV set hooked up in my dressing room. Steve, Bill, and Leonard join me and we watch the game throughout.

There have been tens of thousands of professional baseball games played since we worked on the TV series, but it takes this one with Bill and Leonard present to suddenly transport me ten years to a similar conclave on a *Star Trek* working day during the 1968 World Series. Memories pile upon memories as I flash on what it was like working on the show in those days. Curious, that it is a baseball game of all things that sparks my recall.

Up until this moment I had not asked myself to compare feelings about working on Star Trek then and now. To be sure, in the broad sense both have been enjoyable, but what about the quality of the experience? Was 1968 more or less rewarding, exciting, satisfying than 1978? As the early innings of the game are played out on the screen before me, I find myself reflecting on the early innings of my Star Trek life now long behind me. No question, the television series at its

most stimulating was a high for me that I will not re-
capture on this movie. But this conclusion I have now
reached has less to do with the nature of Star Trek
than it has to do with the nature of Walter Koenig.
Ten years have passed. I am not the same person I was
then. In one real sense, you cannot, you can *never* go
home again because once having had an experience,
you cannot have it again and perceive it the same way.
It's the old "apples and oranges" analogy, only this
time the apples and oranges are the me I was and am.
My frame of reference has changed, I have changed.
I decide, therefore, that I cannot make specific comparisons between old feelings and new ones. Perhaps
that's the reason I haven't tried until now.

I am jolted from my reverie by a whoop from Steve.
The Yankees have gone ahead. I join him pumping
blood double time. The less impassioned members of
our group find our antics a source of amusement, but
what do they know?

4:00 p.m.: This is really turning out to be Steve's day.
Not only do the Yankees win and he wins the baseball
pool, but it is his birthday, too. It is also Persis's birthday, and now two huge cakes are wheeled onto the
set. Everything stops while we each gain a pound and
a half.

Only on a movie set, however, would you find a
publicity man organizing our feast for the best camera
angles. Click-click-click goes Mel. Snap-snap-snap goes
the spontaneity of our celebration.

"All the world's a stage and all the men and women
merely players."

5:48 p.m.: Despite it all, we have made some progress
today. The probe has finally been cooperating and

several takes are in the can. On the set, at least, the future promises to be bright.

TUESDAY, OCTOBER 3

We know all about the laws of probability. The laws of probe-ability are currently being researched on our bridge set. By the time we're finished testing them, we shall have made an important contribution to the literature. Now if we could only wrap up the work sometime before next June.

11:00 a.m.: Franklyn Seales, one of our additional bridge actors, has just announced that the probe really works. No, he doesn't mean that the "effect" is functioning properly, he means that the *probe* is functioning properly. Let me put it to you another way: Franklyn believes that the probe is doing the job it was "sent" to do, that it's tapping into our computers and absorbing all the information. You still don't understand; what he's saying is that the probe is not a creature of imagination but a measurable function of the living presence that hovers beyond our portals. Let me put it to you a fourth way: unbeknownst to us, someone passed out spiked cookies this morning and Franklyn had three.

Emily is a driver and Peggy an electrician. They both work our show. About three years ago the Federal Government pressured the studios into opening up more jobs for women. Time has proven their competence, but I've also wanted to know whether it has led to their acceptance. I'm put in mind of those beer commercials where the guys wear hardhats and exude so much macho that their teeth have muscles. If females exist at all in this world, it is solely to adore the men.

Presumably, the inspiration for these images are the real-life male-dominated blue-collar professions. If that's truly the way it is, then what happens to women when they are force-fed into this environment?

I ask the two young women about their experiences and am surprised to learn that they have been relatively uneventful. To be sure, there was some patronizing and even some downright hostility at the beginning, but that has generally dissipated with time. In its place is cordiality with parameters and a job atmosphere that is bearable, if not fulfilling to its potential. What I distill from their answers, then, is that sexual prejudices still exist and that in proving their worth they have only proved the exception to the rule.

The last question to be answered is: Do those beer commercials and their like simply reflect the society or perpetuate it? If it's the latter, and we all know it is, then they are doing us all a disservice.

2:20 p.m.: Franklyn has come "down." Steps have been taken to ensure that the only hash brownies around hereafter are those made from grated potatoes.

4:19 p.m.: The zeon cylinder continues to make its interminable but inexorable way around the bridge, sucking consoles as it goes. The progress continues to be slow—slower—slowest. Our goal for the day seems to be half a page of story.

5:12 p.m.: I finally get to overhear one of those tight-lipped top-secret conversations between Leonard and Bill:

BILL: Does your makeup itch?
LEONARD: Under my chin.
BILL: Mine, too.
LEONARD: Yeah.

WEDNESDAY, OCTOBER 4

I was wrong; Chekov isn't the only one who gets singed. Today Mr. Spock learns that a probe in the hand is worth third-degree burns.

10:00 a.m.: What can I say after I say "probe"? It's still absorbing information from our data banks.

Because this sequence will be optically augmented in the lab, the reactions the performers are registering are largely to what they *imagine* will be taking place when the effects are animated into the film. The acting term most appropriate to describing this emoting technique is "sense memory." In the absence of the real thing, one calls upon one's memory to recreate visual, audio, kinesthetic—whatever—experiences from other times. The idea is to bring them into such sharp focus that for the actor's purpose they become a present reality to which he can respond. The success of this technique is predicated on the performer's command of his acting "instrument." Command of the acting instrument is based on concentration and the ability to totally involve oneself in the situation—*i.e.,* to block out the real but irrelevant world outside the play.

The real but irrelevant world, however, is the lighting, the camera, the mikes, and two dozen people attending them. When I do not succeed in ignoring these intrusions, my concentration suffers and my imagined environment begins to crack and splinter. When that happens, as it is today, a less lyric, more prosaic—less esthetic, more mundane technique substitutes itself for sense memory; *I make believe*. God, I hope nobody notices!

12:12 p.m.: Robert Wise never ceases to amaze me. Despite his years in the business, his enormous successes, his power and his prestige, he continually evinces as much respect for the people with whom he works as they do for him. I guess when you believe in yourself —better, when you like yourself—all of the psychological garbage that interferes in relationships and causes people to behave at less than their human potential does not exist. Small case in point: we completed a shot that the director deemed satisfactory. I felt I could improve my performance. At most it will last a half-dozen seconds on the screen, but all the same, I asked if we might try it again. He graciously complied.

What next transpired would have been a comedy of errors if time and money were something you could laugh at. For one reason or another (mostly technical breakdowns), we had to reshoot the brief episode again and again. It would have been eminently reasonable for the director to throw up his hands after the fourth or fifth go-round and just decide to stay with the take he had originally found acceptable. To be sure, the difference between what we first got and what I was looking for might be discernible only to me, but having compacted to satisfy my wish, Mr. Wise permitted the camera to roll the ten times it took to get it right.

1:00 p.m.: I've just discovered that Bill spends the lunch hour on Soundstage Ten practicing karate with two professional instructors. I must remember to smile at him more.

4:18 p.m.: I have been waiting all afternoon for the first stunt sequence of the picture. At this point in our story Mr. Spock gets zapped by the probe and does a couple of flying cartwheels across the bridge. When the maneuver is finally performed by Tom Morga, the stuntman doubling for Leonard, I am a trifle disappointed. It just doesn't look that difficult. After the first take I notice that he and Danny, the first assistant, retire to a corner and talk. I already know that the cost of stunts is negotiable depending upon degree of difficulty and danger involved. I now learn that Tom's price, whatever it is, is being determined in the private conversation in progress. The correct procedure is apparently to settle on the price after the first time it is performed on film.

I mention to John L. Black, the key grip and source of this information, that this is a reasonable way to go in a relatively simple stunt like the one just performed, but what if the stunt is so hazardous that it brings into question the likelihood of an after-the-fact negotiation? By way of answer John replies that he has seen stuntmen "eat it" (die) on stunts supposedly as "simple" as this one. He is so impassioned that I am forced to take a second look at Tom's work and re-evaluate it upward. Not only must he go spinning backward and flip over a console without protection for his back, but he must repeat the trick several times since again it is in conjunction with a recalcitrant effect. As for an answer to my question, I must assume that on a stunt where a man drops five thousand feet from an airplane and lands in a haystack, contracts are settled *before* he takes the trip.

5:51 p.m.: As chance would have it, I run into John again as I leave the lot on my way home. We continue our earlier discussion and he relates a story in which a stuntman rolled a car into a river on a movie John was working. It soon became apparent that the man couldn't free himself from the car and was in real trouble. The director, afraid that the shot would be ruined, refused to allow anyone to go in after him. John did, anyway, saving the fellow's life but incurring the wrath of the man in charge. No wonder he feels so strongly about the risks these guys undertake. A thousand pardons, Tom Morga, for minimizing your effort.

THURSDAY, OCTOBER 5

"I have a little shadow that goes in and out with me. . . ." The probe continues to breathe down our necks. In Ilia's case it's a little worse than that, because when it finally does vanish, so does she.

9:20 a.m.: Justice at last. The word has been passed around that George was late for makeup this morning. A lot of grumbling and glowering has followed in his wake because the tardiness means a late start on the first shot of the day. The poor man is totally bewildered by the chill in the air, and no wonder; it wasn't George who was late this morning, it was Walter, but since they're still calling Walter George, it's he who's getting the flak. I love it!

11:08 a.m.: On Monday the probe zapped the security guard, yesterday Mr. Spock got stung, and today it's Ilia's turn. It appears that the whole day will be devoted to this piece of action. Again, an effect is involved here since she has to instantaneously disappear from the bridge after the probe attacks.

An interesting theatrical device is being employed in this sequence, and it has to do with underscoring a dramatic moment by counterpointing it. Ilia disappears in a blinding flash. When the smoke clears all that remains is the tricorder she was holding. The camera focuses on it as it clatters to the floor. To much the same effect that an actor whispers rather than shouts to project the menace of an insane killer, that single tricorder object left behind makes all the more devastating the loss of the person who had been holding it.

To achieve the moment the tricorder has to be suspended in the air and then fall to the deck as Ilia and the blinding flash of the probe vanish. This requires wires, special lighting, and timing, and is not come by easily. As a consequence, it is rehearsed again and again.

11:48 a.m.: We have been shooting all of the probe stuff with 65-mm film and I've been aware that the special camera used is very noisy. There is a barney (muffler) available to deaden the sound, but it has never been attached. For weeks I've been trying to determine why and at the same time wondering how the actors' speeches could be recorded without also recording the loud clickety-clack of the 65-mm camera. I still don't know why the barney isn't employed, but I do have an answer to the second part of my question. The motor noise of the camera will definitely be on the film, and all the footage shot with this instrument will later have to be dubbed on a soundstage.

Despite the fact that I cannot extract from the Abel people an explanation for the missing barney, I cannot conceive that a reasonable one does not exist. Come on, guys, give me the poop. I promise I won't tell anyone.

2:25 p.m.: I have just returned from a costume fitting for a scene that was shot eight days ago—the outfit involved is the sickbay getup for my return to the bridge after being burned. I mentioned to the wardrobe people at the time that a change of costume was in order, but it didn't show up on their charts, and rather than rock the boat, they chose to ignore the information. I considered their response then a solid example of normally functioning bureaucracy. The fact that they have today insisted on fitting me for the costume, anyway, knowing full well that I'll now never appear in it, is a solid example of bureaucracy gone berserk!

3:44 p.m.: I guess I shouldn't feel misused. George, with humor intact, has just described his contribution to today's work. He has been in (sort of) two shots all day. The first called for his likeness to appear in the glass of one of the consoles while the other actors emoted in the foreground. In the second he was asked to take his helm position so that his body would block out a light kicking off an instrument panel. "In the morning I was a reflection, in the afternoon, a shadow," he moaned theatrically.

4:20 p.m.: And the beat goes on. Ilia, for the fourteenth time, gets punished by the probe and again something has gone wrong technically. Even Robert Wise is losing patience. Never one for intemperance, there is, nevertheless, a perceptible glow beneath his collar as he retires to his office.

It's beginning to look now as if George, Nichelle, and I will be in the picture through the first week in November. My five-week guarantee is stretching into thirteen.

5:35 p.m.: Bill tells me about his plans to host a wrap party in December. He intends to buy a hundred tickets to the Rams' last game of the season and invite everyone involved in the film. That's a rather generous offer when you consider the tickets go for twelve bucks apiece.

FRIDAY, OCTOBER 6

The probe and Ilia are gone. Today the crew reacts to their simultaneous disappearance.

10:38 a.m.: Mr. Wise feels compelled to shoot a close-up of Chekov rising from his chair despite the fact that the transpiring events really don't dictate the use of that important angle. The Russian is pretty much a peripheral character during all the reaction stuff and is seen in the master only as a standing background figure. However, the reason he is standing is to block a console that was reflecting light back into the lens (*à la* George), and in the preceding setup Chekov was seated. The aesthetics of continuity require that this transition be documented and, thus, the reason for now registering the rising Russian.

How often has an actor implored the gods for a closeup to record a dynamic performance moment? My wish has been granted, but who would have thought that the gods had such a nasty sense of humor? The closeup is my reaction to Ilia's disappearance. The "dynamic performance moment" is an eyes-blank-mouth-agape look of stupefaction. Oh, gods, you quirky ironic rascals!

The estimated cost of the Rec Deck on which 300 crew members will convene a week from Monday is now $255,000. It's worth every penny of it, or have I already said that I'm passionately in love with this structure?

Under the supervision of Jon Povill, forty new 8-mm tapes have been created for use on the various console viewing screens. That brings the overall total to around one hundred. Not so obviously (since the read-outs are mostly abstract images), what was appropriate for the wormhole is not right for our current crisis. It is a compliment to all concerned that rather than fudge and re-use the old tapes, new ones have been produced at considerable cost. Admittedly, there are times when the production seems to be drowning under the morass of delay, but, always the "good English Soldier," we navigate the bog (as with these new tapes) with élan and style. Plucky devils, these Star Trek people.

We have seen very little of Gene in recent weeks. He pops in for a minute or two every other day and then disappears. It seems his nose is always to the typewriter. It would be nice if he could come onto the set, sit back, and for a little while luxuriate in what he has created. The four makeup artists, the five wardrobe dressers, the sixteen or so actors, the eight dozen carpenters, grips, electricians, engineers, artists, executives, lighting, camera, and special effects people notwithstanding, Star Trek belongs to Gene Roddenberry. It's his baby. As my mother would say, "He should only enjoy."

The first time around, back in 1965–66, there was the conception and the birth with all the concomitant perils a tv series must endure to survive. I suspect that the pains of that labor left little energy for rejoicing during the process of creation. Now, however, in the second coming, the quantity known, the quality assured, this should be a time for Gene to smile broadly, chortle deeply, and say, "Damn, I did that, I'm the one responsible; careers changed, destinies altered, millions influenced, and it all started with me alone, in my mind and never could have in anyone else's."

Today marks the end of the tenth week in what was supposed to have been a twelve-week shooting schedule, and the third act of our story is yet to be rewritten. I guess Gene will have to wait a little longer

yet before he can place the new *Star Trek* on his
bouncing knee.

SUNDAY, OCTOBER 5

*The crew plays the actors today in our final intra-squad
game. Much to my surprise, the attitude among some of
the crew guys borders on contempt. It's only a minority,
but they're making more than their fair share of the
noise. What ensues is the kind of pre-game banter you
find in schoolyards,* grade *schoolyards.*

*It would appear that their mission is to burn the
infidels while ours is to have a good time. From their
point of view it's the real men against the make-believe
men; beer cans and T-shirts against costumes and
pancake. For us the joie de vivre, for them the raison
d'être.*

The joie's win 12 to 5.

MONDAY, OCTOBER 9

*The probe is gone, but not the entity. It has now been
established to be an impossibly huge vessel many thousands of times larger than the* Enterprise *and of a
nature totally unknown to our crew—unknown, that
is, only for the present. The menace of the probe has
been replaced by a new jeopardy. The vessel has seized
us in a tractor beam and is steadily drawing us toward
the iris opening to its interior.*

9:29 a.m.: We have a new navigator. Chief Difalco has
taken over the navigator's post from the absent Lieutenant Ilia. Difalco is played by Marcy Lafferty, Bill

Shatner's wife. It is undeniably true that she got to audition for the role because Bill is in the movie. Nevertheless, she is an actress, not a dilettante, and Robert Wise wouldn't have cast her had she not proven able.

12:11 p.m.: It's been another one of those hurry-up-and-wait mornings. I spend the time talking with Iva, Franklyn, and Ralph Byers. Franklyn's situation is interesting. Here he is doing a bit in our film with barely any lines to say, and at the same time he is up for a starring role in a major motion picture set to roll in November. If he gets the part he will have made a quantum career leap and could very well become hotter and more "important" than any actor in our production.

His circumstances bring to mind the penultimate Hollywood expression of rampaging fear: "Never step on the little guys on the way up; you might meet them on the way down." (*Pen*ultimate, because another actor I know stopped by earlier with a litany of star names who sniff, pop, shoot, and gargle in evidence of the *ultimate* expression of uncontrolled career anxiety.)

Franklyn and Ralph are both recently from New York, and we pass the time talking about the tributes and tribulations of working in the theater. This group is still young, still bound to the stage, not yet totally committed to getting the TV series that will establish their "clout." It's refreshing to listen to them. The juices stir, the blood rages, my passion runneth over with the desire to again work in the theater. George and I have talked in the past about doing a two-character play called *Kataki*. Maybe after the movie is done . . .

1:29 p.m.: Back from lunch and no indication yet when I will begin work. I am told that Jimmy is doing some retakes on Stage Seventeen and I amble over.

Soundstage Seventeen is currently housing both an orbiting dry-dock space office and a travel pod. The action here takes place near the top of our story when Kirk beams from Star Fleet Headquarters on Earth to the space station and meets Scotty for the first time. The particular sequence being reshot today involves Jimmy and a group of extras and is being directed (as second unit work) by Robert Abel.

The scene is M.O.S. (mit-out sound), and Abel is, therefore, able to direct, quite literally, by the numbers. Without sound being recorded, people move back and forth to the director's off-camera voice count from one to eleven. Talk about your science fiction: not only are computers taking over the work of people, but people are now being asked to respond like computers!

Between shots I visit the travel pod tucked away in a corner of the soundstage. The pod is a cruiser that travels at sub-light speed and is used in the story to get Kirk over to the *Enterprise* while repairs are made on the ship's malfunctioning transporter. I take a turn behind the wheel and enter into a brief discussion with Darren Holmes, an apprentice editor on our film, who is also examining the craft.

He confirms what I already suspected about the way Robert Wise films a motion picture. Because he was an editor before he was a director, he cuts the film—so to speak—as he shoots it. Many directors will film a sequence from several different angles and choose which setups they will use *after* viewing them in the editing room. Robert Wise knows in advance exactly how he wants the scene to look and designs his shots with that in mind. As a result, most everything he shoots he uses. There is very little footage for the cutting-room floor. What you see in the dailies is what you get in the finished product.

4:20 p.m.: Back on the bridge. We are being drawn closer and closer to the vessel and then to the opening and then inside. One by one our director calls upon us for reaction shots to this extraordinary turn of events. When he suggests that I improvise a couple of lines to go with my "look," I am so startled (I've become used to just looking) that I find myself protesting their inclusion as being inconsistent with the written word. This is not integrity, this is stupidity. There are precious few opportunities to open my mouth as it is (one of my longest speeches to date remains "AAAARRRRRGGGGGGGHHHHHHHH!") to question this windfall. Fortunately, Mr. Wise asserts his prerogative and I have two more lines to utter.

6:45 p.m.: Dailies today are after work and for the first time in a month I decide to attend. I know that the only Chekov footage will be the rising reaction shot to Ilia's disappearance filmed last Friday. Nevertheless, this kind of acting moment can be deceptively hard to make work. There is no opportunity to get "into" the scene since the scene itself is not being played, only the response to it. Before viewing the dailies I am concerned that my response to the non-existent action was so small that it will not register at all. After watching myself on the big screen, however, it now seems to me that it was not to a simple disappearance that I was reacting but to a direct hit on my sinuses scored by several thousand volts of electricity. Such faces! Such carrying on!

I sink down deep into my chair and consider the feasibility of crawling under the carpet and slithering out of the projection room unnoticed.

I should have made that a month and a day without viewing dailies.

TUESDAY, OCTOBER 10

*It is rabbit holes, not wormholes or black holes, I'm
thinking of today as we pass through the iris of the
vessel. The vast chamber, the* Enterprise *enters, with
its power-field walls and erupting energy displays, is
like a futuristic successor to Alice's wonderland.*

7:40 a.m.: The Lewis Carroll story along with an
evaluation of our film run through my head as I drive
to the studio this morning. Although I have already
perceived a similarity between that work and our adventure, it is, curiously, an area of difference between
the two that seems more important to me now.

Alice in Wonderland is fantasy; *Star Trek* is science
fiction. There is a built-in detachment for the reader/
viewer in addressing himself to the fantasy genre. The
"fantastic" elements in such stories do, by their nature,
inhibit personal involvement. Science fiction, particularly when it is speculative fiction, presumes possibility,
implies a future reality, and, therefore, encourages
identification on the part of its audience. If the reader/
viewer believes in the situation, he is more apt to
become its captive. Every good movie has its own
tractor beam—one that pulls the viewing public along
with it.

How well we succeed in involving our audience will
determine how well we will succeed as a motion picture.

The third, last, and climactic act of our story begins
just after we enter the vessel. If anything, from here
on out our story will be more dynamic and compelling
than before. On the other hand, if we haven't hooked
the viewer by now, it will all go for nothing. No wonder, then, that on this particular day as we begin the

last third of our film, I find myself preoccupied with questions concerning our audience appeal. Don't misunderstand, I am very encouraged by what has transpired to date, but I cannot be certain that my head and not my heart is the chief reason. However, even if I cannot objectively evaluate the factors necessary for our success, I do, at least, know what they are: (1) the director, the writers, and the actors must establish the credibility of the premise. If we are successful, the audience accepts as its own the reality we fashion; (2) the art and special effects units must take that reality and transform it into a heightened and unforgettable sensory experience. If factors 1 and 2 do not work in concert, success will not be achieved. Without faith in the story and characters, art becomes veneer and effects simply fireworks. Without the imagination and skill to properly render the visuals, the story and its people are made to appear less than they are.

All this I'm thinking as I pull into my parking space and begin the walk toward my dressing room.

Let's see, as I recall in the Carroll story, Alice was made to feel very anxious by mad hatters and vanishing cats. In our story, if my heart is where my head is, it'll be the audience as well as the *Enterprise* crew that tumbles down a rabbit hole, passes through an iris into a world never before created on film, and experiences an anxiety attack close to the level of dissociation.

8:13 a.m.: In the makeup room. Charlie Schram informs me that my eyelashes hang low in the corner of my eye. (No wonder my career hasn't skyrocketed!) I could make my eyes appear larger, he tells me, by curling my lashes up. Curling my lashes?! You mean with one of those things women use?! What would the kids on the block say . . . ? Holy cow, I know what they'd say . . . ! I'd never be allowed back in the old neighborhood. Banished forever. Excommunicated from my childhood by the holy ordinance of "J.J." and "Lefty." Never mind I haven't flipped bubble-gum cards or played stickball in thirty years, I've got to keep my options open. . . . No . . . No . . . Stay back. . . . Stay . . . bbaaacccckkkkk!

Too late. Charlie insists upon demonstrating. I examine the results: disgusting—that's the only word for it. I mean, what am I, a peacock or an actor? So what if it makes my eyes look bigger? So what if for the first time they're open wide enough to fully expose my sensitive soul? So what that now my career will probably skyrocket. So what . . . Ah, the hell with it. Once I applied the cucumber slices, my fate was sealed. Besides, I think "Lefty" is now a transvestite, "J.J." a dentist, and all the good stickball bats are broken, anyway.

Last night on Stage Twenty-seven Robert Wise interviewed 500 of the most intense, fervent, and committed Star Trek fans in the Western Hemisphere. They were there as supplicants for the roles of crew people in next week's Rec Deck scene. Damn, I wish I had been there. Think of the religious significance: not a Volkswagen ride to Paramount, but a pilgrimage to Mecca. Not a cattle call, but a convening of the Twelve Tribes. Not a soundstage, but a cathedral. Not a director, but a guru. Not sixty-dollars-a-day salary, but a benediction. "And he looketh down uponeth his flock and spaketh unto them, 'You have achieved nirvana.' "

11:15 a.m.: New pages. Chekov has been cut from a scene in which he was to accompany Kirk in investigation of an intruder. The intruder, it turns out, is a mechanical unit that looks exactly like the vanished Ilia—except that it isn't wearing any clothes. Naturally, Persis plays the replica as well. This is the nude scene she protested against doing. I now understand she will be permitted to wear a body stocking.

Holding the Chekov-less pages, I feel depression driving past my kneecaps on the way toward total envelopment. It's bad enough I'm claustrophobic and panic under the restraint of tight quarters, but being trussed and blanketed by low spirits adds insult to injury, certification to suspicion, psychosis to neurosis.

In the final analysis, I think maybe I should have followed my very first impulses and devoted my life to selling ice cream from a Good Humor truck.

4:22 p.m.: The bridge. The scene they've been trying to get for an hour involves dialogue and action between Kirk, Spock, and Decker after the iris closes behind the *Enterprise* and the ship is sucked deeper into the bowels of the monstrously large vessel.

It starts out as Kirk and Decker, tense and silent, watch the viewscreen from the upper deck of the bridge. At the same time, Spock, with his back to them, sits at his science console punching up read-outs that will hopefully give some clue to the nature of the antagonist.

The scene progresses as Spock volunteers the data he is accumulating and ends up with Kirk and Spock crossing into the elevator while Decker descends the two stairs to the captain's chair and assumes the conn.

The setup dictates that the camera first truck forward into a tight three-shot of the stationary men and then dolly back to pick up more area as the two officers enter the elevator and the third takes over the command post.

The shot is a long time coming because of the movement of the camera and the accompanying focus and lighting problems it engenders. After a half-dozen rehearsals they are ready to shoot, and after a half-dozen takes they feel they are *getting close* to one they can print.

Fatigue has begun to set in and everyone is looking heavenward when they roll the camera one more time. Suddenly there is a new hangup. Darrell Pritchett is the special effects man who stands behind the camera and presses the buttons on stage that light the bulbs offstage that cue the technicians behind the set to activate the various rear-screen-projected panel effects that the actors don't operate themselves. Everyone is tired and Darrell is no exception. He's off in his timing.

The scene is rehearsed again and then shot again, and, again, Darrell's thumb is slow. By now there is much grumbling and more than a little evil eyeing of the usually expert effects operator. Robert Wise points a threatening finger at the harassed man and accuses him of driving him, through frustration, back to his bag of Fritos. He storms off in mock anger to some accompanying laughter, but in his wake clouds of impatience and discontent form again. A look to Darrell confirms the suspicion that the pressure is getting to him.

Robert Wise returns and they try again. This time everything goes smoothly until the very end, when Kirk and Spock approach the elevator doors. Then, just as in the old blooper reels, they don't open on time and the two actors go crashing into them chin first. Guess who is supposed to push the button to cue the backstage elevator operator?

There are some giggles but even more strain. The atmosphere on the set is growing electric. You can just about feel the crackling. One wayward spark and there is going to be an explosion.

I am sitting close by for an off-camera line and praying that we'll get through the shot this time. I am convinced that something very unpleasant will happen if we don't. Somebody is going to blow up and our compatible group will suffer the fallout. There has not been one overt display of temper in the two months we've been working on this set. I've considered that harmony an ingredient to our success. I remember Doug, our second A.D., saying that he had never worked on a production that matched this one for genuine warmth and congeniality. I took pride in that statement then. I take pride in it now. I don't want to see anyone embarrassed. I don't want to see anyone humiliated. I want the façade to reflect the substance. If we have a terrific picture, I want it to be because we have a terrific group working together terrifically.

They begin again. Kirk and Decker watch the viewscreen. Our tension behind the camera is more than an equal to theirs in front of it. It is supposed to be quiet after the camera starts rolling, but it is more than that now. We hold our collective breaths waiting for the first dialogue line that will prompt the first camera move and cue the first read-outs on the science console. I stare straight ahead. I particularly don't want to look at Darrell. Why the hell doesn't Bill begin?! The wait seems interminable.

At last Kirk starts his speech and . . . behind him the elevator doors suddenly fly open. There is a long beat of dead silence as we try to recover from the shock of the empty elevator opening for absolutely no reason. And then the moment passes and laughter, full-throated with relief, floods the bridge. We are helpless in the undertow, drowning in it. What a glorious way to go. What might have turned ugly has turned special. We are sharing, coming together. Each person's laughter seems to incite that of the others. It builds and builds. No one seems to care if it never stops. When Darrell pressed the switch for the elevator instead of the console, he also pressed us closer together. I believe that,

I truly do. The incident may be forgotten with time, but its effect will remain. Darrell will forever after be a major celebrity in our company, and our company will forever after be just a little bit better than it was before.

WEDNESDAY, OCTOBER 11

Kirk and Spock intercept the nude Ilia unit (can a machine be nude?) in the officers' quarters and learn from it/her that the vessel out there calls itself V'ger.

8:50 a.m.: "Ego is not real. Ego is only an idea. You have as to whom you think you are. Why not drop all identity; then there is nothing to defend?"

I don't know what it means, either, but it definitely sounds profound. It certainly is different from the graffiti generally found on john walls—which, of course, answers the question posed by wise men the world over: Yes, even the toilets on the *Star Trek* set are of a higher order.

9:11 a.m.: At last, a logical explanation for the absence of a barney on the 65-mm camera as told to me by the Robert Abel camera operator. The reason a barney is not used to deaden the sound on the 65-mm camera is because the barney used on the 65-mm camera doesn't deaden the sound.

9:45 a.m.: Another angle on yesterday's scene where Kirk and Spock exit. In the first rehearsal when Kirk tells Decker he has the conn, Steve steps smartly forward and then suddenly drops to his knees, wrapping the Captain's chair in a bear hug while blubbering, "At last, it's mine, it's mine!"

Bill, responding like a true commander, stamps his foot petulantly and screams, "I change my mind, I change my mind!"

10:22 a.m.: I find out why Chekov was written out of the scene in the officers' quarters where the Ilia unit first appears. The pages I had were from the original movie-for-television script that was supposed to have been shot last year. At that point Leonard had not come aboard the production and it was felt that Chekov, as head of security, was the logical choice to accompany Kirk. Obviously, in the current version, with Mr. Spock present, it is equally logical that the red pencil would come out and the Russian lieutenant with it. Oh, well, there's always the sequel.

11:19 a.m.: One last shot and we leave the bridge for a couple of days. On an order from Kirk, Chekov orders a security team to accompany Kirk and Spock in investigating the intruder.

I've been trying to get an inversion of the letters *v* and *w* into the Russian's speech whenever appropriate, and each time Tom Overton, the sound mixer, tells Robert Wise that it comes over too confusingly. I make one last effort now: "Security team to main elevwaters."

"Cut!" comes the off camera response. "Let's try it again, Walter," our keen-eared director says with a forbearance generally reserved for dealings with the mentally defective. Jeez, you can't blame a guy for trying.

11:30 a.m.: It's a "wrap" on the bridge set. The crew is moving toward the officers' quarters. I'm moving toward the exit. I'll be off for the rest of the week. Two and one-half days away from the set. I wonder when the withdrawal pains will begin.

SATURDAY, OCTOBER 14

A one-day Star Trek convention in El Paso. It should go well; no college football games, no rodeos, no square dances, no competition. Question: So how come only 700 people show up? Answer: There is a "menudo" dining celebration in town. For the uninitiated, that translates as coming in second to a "cow's-intestines cook-off." And here I thought I was irresistible...

MONDAY, OCTOBER 16

Today we back-pedal 59 pages to the Recreation Deck scenes. It will be one of the few times we have shot out of sequence. It is here that Kirk tells the crew of the Enterprise *the nature of its mission while they watch on the viewscreen the havoc wrought by the unknown (at this point) adversary.*

8:45 a.m.: The Rec Deck is now complete on Soundstage Eight and it is there we assemble this morning. The "we" has more weight behind it than usual. In addition to our regular group, there are 300 new crew people. Of this body, 100 are male Star Trek fans and 25 are female Star Trek fans. The rest, with a few notable exceptions, are members of the Screen Extras Guild. Among the notable exceptions are Robert Wise's wife, Millicent (a devoted follower of the old series),

Susan Sackett, Rosanna Attias, Barbara Minster (hair-dresser), and Ve Neill (makeup artist). They all look quite smashing in their new regulation uniforms.

10:11 a.m.: A truly choice of extemporaneous moment: it is the initial rehearsal of Kirk's entrance into the huge hall. The sequence picks up with the large crew contingent watching the viewscreen before the Captain's arrival. They are instructed by our director to react to the devastation he is describing (the viewscreen action will be added post-production) with chagrin and apprehension. They are further directed to anticipate Kirk's entrance under these circumstances with somber foreboding. The indoctrination completed, they now turn—fists clenched, jaws sets, eyes grave—toward the wings as their intense leader enters. It is Bill's first time on the set this morning, but he moves forward confidently and totally in character.

A befitting hush falls over the room as he mounts the platform from which he will address the ship's complement. He momentarily sorts his feelings, searching for the words with which to describe the nature of their mission and the danger that lies before them. At last his shoulders heave and he takes a deep breath. The air puffs in his cheeks unexpelled, however, because suddenly, without warning, the hall erupts in prolonged and enthusiastic applause. Gone, along with the Captain's dire announcement, is the director's caution to play the scene with solemnity. Instead, spontaneously, and led no doubt by the 125 Star Trek fans, the entire roomful of people have given sound to their affection for the redoubtable Captain of the *Enterprise*. Bill has no choice but to break character and take a bow.

There are five different sets of camera crews operating in the Rec Deck. Four of the groups are recording the action for the *Star Trek* movie and the fifth one, an outfit called Continental Films, is recording the recording of the action for a film on the making of the making of the *Star Trek* movie. (What we need, of course, is one more crew shooting the Continental group for a film on the making of the making of the making of the *Star Trek* movie. That way, we'll ensure the return of our negative cost and make all the Pirandello fans out there happy, too.)

A second camera crew is shooting the scene at floor level from a single angle, but it's the three other camera groups that I find most interesting. They are mounted one over the other in uneven increments at the front of the hall. The lowest camera is designated the "A" camera, the middle one the "mat" camera, and the highest one, on top of a camera crane, the "top" camera. (A literary bent is not a requisite for operating a motion picture camera.)

There is so much room to cover and so many people to include that it is necessary to do so from three different elevations. Mounting them one directly above the other maintains a reasonably constant point of view and makes cutting between different angles in the editing room an easier job.

We were not able to use multiple cameras concurrently on the bridge because of the very special lighting employed there. A second camera even a few inches distant would record hot spots and shadows differently and cause the results to have a different "look" from one cut to another. Here in the Rec Deck, the lighting is very bright and even and the matching problem does not exist to the same degree.

The mat camera has a whole other interesting function as well. This is the 65-mm machine operated by the Robert Abel company. Its implementation here is due to the fact we have no ceiling on this set. The majority of the lights illuminating the proceedings are hung from above, making a ceiling impractical. However, we do need a ceiling because the wide angles being used would reveal one in the picture.

To compensate for this problem, the upper portion of the mat camera lens has been blocked out so that only that part of the film recording the floor action is exposed. After the sequence is shot, this film, referred to as the "master," is removed from the camera and stored undeveloped. A second magazine shooting the same action with the same blacked-out lens is developed and becomes the work print.

A painting of the ceiling is then matched up with the work print and tested again and again until it can be matted into the unexposed area of the Rec Deck film with color and light consistent from one to the other. When this is accomplished the mat lines between the ceiling painting and Rec Deck proper will be undetectable. With the work print as the frame of reference, the master copy is then reinserted into the camera. Now the lens is blacked out on the bottom half while the top half is recording the ceiling. When the film is at last printed, a covered Rec Deck appears on the screen with no way to detect that it is not all one structure.

11:30 a.m.: I am talking with a fellow named Bert who is a production director for the effects company. I learn from him that in Abel's employ and assigned to this production are people who have worked on *2001, Star Wars,* and *Close Encounters of the Third Kind.* I ask him if he thinks that the effects the optical company will finally come up with will be innovative. In response, his voice takes on a timbre and resonance that has me rocking on my heels. "I don't *think* it will be innovative—I damn well know it will be. Nothing like what we are doing has ever been seen before in a motion picture!" Bert's demeanor is very impressive. With this man playing a leading part in Abel's effort, I feel renewed confidence in that company's ability to succeed on our behalf.

11:49 a.m.: Alas, the aura of an anonymity that seems to follow me again raises its nondescript head. With its appearance the giddy euphoria my conversation with Bert stimulated is replaced by a new feeling: one most accurately described as homicidal mania. This time the *nom de guerre* by which I am addressed is not "George" instead of Walter or even "Charlie" (used so cloyingly by Danny McCauley because of my baggy pants). No, this time instead of Walter, the new camera operator among us says, "Will the fellow *standing in* for Bill Shatner move a little to his left?"

The *Enterprise* has not yet lifted off at the time of this scene, and behind the Rec Deck extending its width can be seen a huge background painting of the dry dock. When viewed from specific angles at the head of the room, it appears that the Rec Deck, as part of the *Enterprise,* is housed *within* the dry-dock painting. The interesting thing to me is that the mammoth canvas was designed and painted to be filmed from only two perspectives. Should another camera angle be tried, the illusion of depth would be lost and the two-dimensional flat mural would appear to be just that.

Franklyn has just informed me that he got the starring role he was up for in that major motion picture. The film is *The Onion Field* and the role is that of Jimmy Smith. I feel absolutely prophetic. Way back in August I was talking about our very talented crew of young bridge actors and how I was sure that with time they would rise above their current professional status. Franklyn is now on his way, climbing toward a "star" quite different but no less luminous than the ones the *Enterprise* voyages past.

This is the first time I've worked with Jimmy Doohan since we started shooting. Actually, I had not thought we'd work together at all until the final bridge scene in the movie. The script never did delineate which of the crew would be assembled for this sequence, and for some reason I just assumed he would be stoking in the engine room while the rest of us were stocking the Rec Deck. "Working together" now is little more than an occasional look from one to the other and a grave nod exchanged between us. Captain Kirk has the spoken lines here. The rest of us have only the lines that come from furrowed brows.

Grace Lee Whitney is also on hand. This is a first for us. We have never before appeared in a scene together. Mainly because we have never before appeared in Star Trek together.

I've just learned that the estimated cost of shooting two days in the Rec Deck is $210,000.

2:30 p.m.: Paramount has reinstated its strictest security precautions while we are working on this set: absolutely no visitors on Stages Eight and Nine. The prohibition to the former is because we have over 300 people present now and guests would simply add to the monumental onstage traffic problems. Stage Nine is off limits because there is concern that among the very enthusiastic Star Trek fans engaged here there might be one or more tempted to take home a memento from the bridge or engine room.

I find this reasoning a bit unfair. After all, would a true disciple lift the crucifix from the altar at St. Peter's?

3:10 p.m.: I am asked by Iva the reason for the intense partisanship of Star Trek fandom. There is, of course, the reasons that motivate the vast majority of the show's enthusiasts. They include good stories, dimensional characterizations, interesting relationships, scientific integrity, hope for the future, and enlightened philosophical positions. These explanations address themselves to the intrinsic elements of the Star Trek formula, and, as such, their effectiveness can be calculated on a rather simple arithmetic table. In other words, the better the story, the more interesting the relationships, the greater the response from the audience.

There is, however, another less obvious, more significant explanation for the show's popularity in certain quarters. It is my experience that among Star Trek's most militant and passionate devotees, there is a segment who derive psychological succor from their allegiance. Frequently these are people with a weak self-image for whom identification with the show is a means to the popularity, respect, love that they feel is missing in their lives.

This kind of psychological fallout effect is by no means limited to this small portion of the Star Trek population. Any rabid fan, whether it be of a television series, a sports team, an entertainer, or a political figure, who casts himself in the shadow of another, who sacrifices personal achievement to root for someone else's success, is certainly quartered in the same ego bag as those orally compensatory Star Trek fans who are consumed by their loyalty to Kirk, Spock, *et al.*

4:30 p.m.: The shooting is going very smoothly. The non-union extras (S.T. fans) will finish today. The camera angles employed tomorrow will be from tighter positions, requiring fewer people to fill the camera lens. There is a little grumbling among some of the fans. A couple have flown in from New York and Philadelphia, several from other parts of the country, and now too soon the cherished daydream is over. All the same, I doubt if there is one who would have chosen to miss this experience had he/she to do it over.

TUESDAY, OCTOBER 17

The Rec Deck congregation continues to react to the destructive power of the adversary shown on the viewscreen and to their Captain's instructions regarding the Enterprise's mission. Kirk's last words before he leaves the hall is to inform the crew that the pre-launch countdown will begin in forty minutes.

9:27 a.m.: Whoops! It now appears that I spoke too soon about crucifixes and artifacts. Doug Wise tells me that one of the young ladies who worked yesterday purloined her loincloth—a pair of uniform slacks is missing. I would have sworn that no one would have tried that. All the same, I hope she gets to keep them.

I am also told that among the 500 people interviewed for the crew positions were a couple of great-grandmas. When one was asked to explain her presence, she was overheard to reply that "hope springs internal." Whether she was seeking an anatomical source for her enthusiasm or just malapropping, she gets my vote for Star Trek fan of the year.

The departure of the fan extras has left a small black hole of its own in our production. With them has gone an uninhibited excitement, a refreshing ingenuousness that becomes a conscious longing-for only through its absence. It's sort of like not knowing what you've been missing until you're given a taste of it. Today we have only the professional extras and our professional selves, and because of that the Rec Deck seems a little less like a room aboard the *Enterprise* and a bit more like a movie set on a soundstage. Don't get me wrong, I still love this massive chamber, I just wish that great-grandma could be hanging in there today at the front of the pack.

3:15 p.m.: A lot of scurrying about. A definite touch of tension in the air. No wonder, we're being invaded! Unlike anything we've ever seen before in our world: gray suits, gray ties, gray eyes, they come from the place of grayness. A place incomprehensible, beyond our ken, where no Star Trek person has gone before. They come from the book of ledgers speaking strange mystical words like "box office" and "rental fees" and "money players." They are known as the DISTRIBUTORS and silently they observe us and silently they move on carrying their gray attaché cases and thinking their gray thoughts.

5:25 p.m.: The last of the actors is released. A few of the extras remain. One more shot, two at most, and the work here is complete. The hall will stand empty again. This time not even the echoing blows of a solitary carpenter to disturb the silence. All that will remain are after-images, brief incomplete memories of two short days. Not enough time to make this marvelous place our own. How many days on the bridge has time moved laboriously, has not moved at all? And now it rushes past—a temptress, exciting our imaginations but offering only a grazing kiss. Perfidy, thy name is time.

Fact mirrors fancy. The *Enterprise* has moved back and forth in time in various episodes of the series and so does this production. The company now leaves this early period of our story and returns to the present. For the next several days Robert Wise will be shooting in Ilia's quarters and in the Medical Examining Room. It is here they will learn that the Ilia unit is a probe sent out by *V'ger* and that it is composed of micro-miniature hydraulics, molecule-sized multi-processor chips and an osmotic micro-pump. But you already knew that.

What I know is that I will be off during this time. My return is slated for Monday. I'm guessing Wednesday.

SUNDAY, OCTOBER 22

11:00 a.m.: Our first softball game against a league opponent is with "Grandpa Goes to Washington." It's only a practice affair and won't count in the standings but should give us some idea of our strengths and weaknesses.

1:30 p.m.: I pitch and "hold" them to six runs. (I now know what one of our weaknesses is.) Fortunately, their pitcher isn't any better. We end in a tie.

There are about two dozen fans in the stands rooting us home. If we don't actually destroy their faith in our omnipotence, we bend it a lot. Never mind, it was fun.

TUESDAY, OCTOBER 24

Back to blue-screening and a short side trip to the planet Vulcan.

10:00 a.m.: The whole morning, it appears, will be devoted to shooting blue-screen footage. Originally it was hoped that each such process shot could be filmed in sequence as it appeared in the story. However, tech-

nical problems have complicated these setups and se-
verely taxed our time schedule. It was decided, therefore,
that at a designated interval all of the blue-screen shots
not at that point recorded would be done together. The
designated interval is now and will be on and off for
the next couple of days.

The first of these sequences to be filmed are pickups
from the dreaded "wormhole." When we worked on
this episode way back in August, there were a few
blue-screen setups, but mainly the camera faced the
crew and registered what was happening to them. Now
the camera is exclusively at the actors' backs, shooting
past them and out toward the huge bank of fluorescent
lights. Even though it is only a shoulder here, an ear
there, that is in the picture, here we go all over again
at 24 and 48 frames per second, bouncing and swaying
as we get sucked deeper and deeper into the whirlpooling abyss.

10:57 a.m.: De Forest stops by my dressing room between shots. We begin talking about the Australian
pilot who disappeared over the weekend shortly after
reporting that he was being approached by a UFO.

In the course of our conversation, De relates an interesting story. Way back in 1950 while driving over
flatlands toward Montgomery, Alabama, he, his wife,
Carolyn, and a friend observed a jet-propelled, cigar-
shaped craft in the sky that had all the design trappings
of something extraterrestrial. Despite knowing that the
local Montgomery papers carried other eyewitness reports of it the next day, De felt sure he would not be
believed and for years never talked about it. He finally
did relate the experience at a Star Trek convention
sometime back and was afterward approached by a
UFO investigator for the government who had been in
the audience and was familiar with the sighting he men-

tioned. To De's surprise, the man told him that the phenomenon had been documented and officially confirmed as a genuine unidentified flying object.

I remember seeing some kind of rapidly moving spheroid shape outside my window one night when I was ten years old. Listening to De now, I am suddenly convinced that *every one* of the Star Trek regulars has had a similar experience. *Why won't they listen?! Why won't they see what it means?! We're not just any eight or nine actors. We're special. We have been touched! It is our responsibility through Star Trek to bring our world into contact with other worlds. WE ARE THE CHOSEN! !*

It's amazing how those blue lights can get to you after a while.

11:28 a.m.: It is important that the composition of the scenes now being shot is consistent with those filmed back in August. To this end the editing table is back on the soundstage showing us the footage recorded earlier. What we look at now is quite different from what we saw in the dailies and even different from what we saw in the brief spliced footage this machine has shown us before. Preliminary editing has been done and sound effects incorporated. We are now looking at a story that has continuity and duration. The effect is startling. Even on the small editing table screen the action is absorbing and dynamic. I find myself viewing it anew, virginally, experiencing it for the first time. My God, if forty-five seconds of the picture can do this, what can we expect from the finished work! *Beyond* what we can imagine is the hopeful answer I supply myself.

1:35 p.m.: An exterior Vulcan set has been completed at the "B" tank on the Paramount lot. It is sandwiched in between set pieces for other shows being filmed at the studio. Ironically, it is exactly where the waterfront was located on the "Barbary Coast" TV series that Bill starred in a few years ago. The company now moves to this site for some Vulcan footage of Mr. Spock. This sequence, like that of the Rec Deck, takes place earlier but is being photographed now because the set has only just now been erected.

The scene in progress has Spock on his knees in contemplation amidst ancient Vulcan ruins. Overhead the camera moves back and forth on a crane recording the action. If it were to move just another sixty degrees to the right, it would pick up the general store, barns, hitching posts, etc., of "Little House on the Prairie." Who says farmers and Vulcans can't be friends?

5:11 p.m.: We return to the bridge for more blue-screen bouncing as the *Enterprise* begins its pull out from the wormhole. Gadzooks! Bill and Steve have been released for the day and it's too late to bring them back now. We can't continue without them. We're going to have to make it a wrap. This is the first time this particular problem has occurred and is just one more cause for frustration.

"I want this shot at 8:30 tomorrow morning," declares our director forcefully. In a situation like this you go with the favorite. I'm betting we'll have it by 8:29.

WEDNESDAY, OCTOBER 25

You've heard of the blue meanies? Well, we got 'em, again and again and again. I wonder what it was like shooting Star Trek *before we had to look at that damn screen. I can't remember back that far.*

8:45 a.m.: The shot ordered by our director late yesterday afternoon is now in the can. A remarkable achievement considering our penchant for delayed starts.

10:11 a.m.: Just to keep the record straight, I've just learned that the missing costume from the Rec Deck scene wasn't taken, after all. Rosanna had been the one dressed in it. She wore it back to her office in the *Star Trek* building that evening and changed into her civvies there. She returned it promptly the following day but I didn't find out about it until now. I told you Star Trek fans don't steal.

The most current scuttlebutt around Stage Nine has Paramount contemplating sponsorship of the largest Star Trek convention ever attempted. It would include the dismantling and reassembling of *all* our sets at some public arena like the L.A. Convention Center. No confirmation about it from anybody, but enough idle chatter to make one wonder. It would be one hell of a publicity stunt at that, wouldn't it?

1:40 p.m.: We have been awaiting a decision as to whether the company will return this afternoon to "B" tank and the planet Vulcan. The decision has now come down to postpone the move to a sunnier day. So back to the blue screen and the Reuben shirt. The wormhole is once more behind us and we are now doing the blue-screen shots of the entity's approach.

2:38 p.m.: Things are not going too well. It is very difficult to employ the actors in any setup where the blue screen is turned on. The screen is back-lit (the curtain is draped over and in front of the lights) and the blue color is spilling onto the bridge and washing over the actors. Since space, for one thing, isn't blue, and for another doesn't reflect color, the value of the screen is greatly diminished. Finally, in some exasperation, Robert Wise clears the set of all the actors and decides to shoot the screen from the point of view of the different crew members on the bridge. Shooting from the actor's P.O.V. instead of using angles that include them eliminates the need for bodies in the composition of the picture. We are banished to our dressing rooms.

3:11 p.m.: The first twenty-two pages of the rewritten third act have come down from the front office. There is a lot less bridge action now than in the first draft, but, not so curiously, I actually have a few more lines than before. After Chekov was red-penciled from the scene in Ilia's quarters, I called Gene and explained that said deletion made infinitesimal the Russian's contribution to the rest of the story. Gracious, as usual, he promised to look at the rewriting then in progress with an eye out for Chekov's welfare.

3:45 p.m.: Gene has come by the set. I am about to thank him for his effort on my behalf, but he looks so preoccupied, so distressed, that instead I simply press his arm in greeting. He returns the salutation silently as if grateful that I not engage him in small talk at this particularly troublesome time. I watch him go, sensing that I have only seen the exposed tip of the fathoms-deep pressure he must be under to produce the Act Three pages to everyone's satisfaction.

Not only must the work be compatible with the esthetic tastes of Paramount, Robert Wise, and Gene's co-writer, Harold Livingston (no doubt all of whose tastes are at some point in opposition to each other), but he must now consider the preferences of Bill and Leonard. Due to contractual stipulations based in part on the length of the shooting schedule, the two actors now also have script approval. Nobody ever promised Gene a rose garden, but the question is: Can orchids, tulips, and narcissuses grow together in the same ground?

For his part, Robert Wise must also be experiencing considerable agitation. The last time, I am told, that he didn't have a completed script in his hands on the first day of shooting was for *Run Silent, Run Deep*, and that was over twenty years ago!

4:25 p.m.: George and I have another of our conversations about the consuming nature of our Star Trek identification. He tells of being recently elected vice-president of the Department of Human Resources—a prestigious national lobbying organization—and of being approached afterward by well-wishers who seemed at least equally interested in acquiring Lieutenant Sulu's autograph as they were in congratulating him.

4:48 p.m.: They're still shooting the blue screen without actors. I climb the stairs to the art department and sit with a couple of veteran employees who pass a flask and reminisce about the old days. The names bandied about are the stuff of legends: Bogart, Selznick, Chaplin, Goldwyn, Cooper. On a day when we can't get our act together in the future, the past lives and breathes before my very eyes.

5:35 p.m.: I am called back to the set. All the other principals have been dismissed, but they need another one of those silent reaction shots from me. If "acting is reacting," as drama teachers are heard to fervently declare, then I am certainly the personification of the craft at the apogee of its nobility. Look, I've got to find some reason why I'm still here while everyone else is at home with a warm bowl of chicken soup.

THURSDAY, OCTOBER 26

V'ger, with us inside it, is on a course into Earth's orbit. We're less than three and a half hours away. Spock has left the ship through airlock four.

7:45 a.m.: Another early call. It's starting to become a habit. There is much buzzing about the new pages while we get our makeup applied. The feeling is that the script is tighter but that we don't have a lock on it yet. There are three main story points that have to be resolved in the third act: (1) What is the significance (philosophically) of *V'ger* and how is its threat to Earth to climax? (2) How is Spock, so far troubled and distant, to come to terms with himself? (3) How shall the relationship between Decker and Ilia culminate, and what is to become of them?

These story points have, of course, all been dealt with in the various drafts to date. It now requires that they be made to interrelate and play off each other within a solid story structure and for the purpose of having a dynamic and satisfying ending to the film.

12:12 p.m.: We are shooting the first of the new bridge pages for the third act. Sulu, Uhura, and Chekov are relaying the data they are receiving from their consoles to the Captain. The element of time, used frequently as a tension builder on the TV series, is being similarly employed here. Uhura reports that *V'ger* is fast approaching Earth. The implication is that if we are to stop it, we must do it soon.

We are one shot away from finishing the sequence when we break for the noon meal. After lunch the company will regroup at "B" tank for the remaining footage of Vulcan. All the bridge actors are dismissed for the day except those involved in the shipboard piece left over from the morning. "Those" actors is me.

1:30 p.m.: With nearly four hours to kill before we return to the interior set, I decide to go home. I can't be bothered about getting in and out of the Reuben shirt again, so I wear my uniform home.

The enormity of what I have done doesn't occur to me until I am on the freeway well along toward my destination. A passing car swerves perilously close to my left front fender and I react by swinging wide to avoid a collision. I have compensated too much and have faded into the slow lane, already occupied by a laundry truck. Again I twist the wheel and am now careening back and forth across the freeway like waltzing mice. A motorcyclist barely gets out of my way and now the wire fence along the inside lane is scraping paint from my fender. When I finally get myself straightened out, I realize that through all of the preceding danger I was flashing on the fact that I was still in my *Star Trek* costume. Never mind the recklessness on the road; the recklessness of not taking off my Reuben blouse is what truly has me shaking. Paramount has this tremendous investment in the *Star Trek* motion picture and is understandably concerned that a favorable public image be maintained regarding the product.

And here I am getting myself killed with the resulting carnage plastered, no doubt, across the newspaper pages of the late editions. A bloodied *Enterprise* uniform shrouding a battered corpse would not reflect positively on the *Star Trek* motion picture.

I know what you're thinking, and I'm thinking it, too. How could my first feelings be of guilt for my wardrobe transgression and not fear for my mortal being? You're absolutely right, I'm absolutely nuts!

4:00 p.m.: The effects of my brush with death have at last set in and I motor back to the studio at a grandfatherly 35 miles per hour. The piece to be filmed is the reverse on an angle over Chekov's shoulder toward Kirk, done this morning.

My legs are still shaking as I step into my Russian accent and apprehensively announce that the console data points to a new jeopardy for the *Enterprise.*

My anxiety is very convincing, says the director afterward.

The latest schedule breakdown (alas, it keeps breaking down) has the company filming sequences between Decker and the Ilia unit and between Spock, Kirk, and McCoy for the next eight days. Since all these scenes take place away from the bridge, I shall not be needed. Nevertheless, I think I shall come by on at least one of my free days. Perhaps, free of eyeliner, I shall see things differently on the set.

SUNDAY, OCTOBER 29

Our last practice softball game before opening day. Our opposition is the "Laverne and Shirley" team. The girls don't show up, but everyone else does, and most of

*them cross the plate. I give up thirteen runs. For-
tunately, we score nineteen. I think we're ready to play
the Yankees.*

TUESDAY, OCTOBER 31

The Ilia unit explains that V'ger's *purpose is to "survive."*

10:00 a.m.: Happy Halloween! This is the one day of
the year that Mr. Spock goes unnoticed on Melrose
Avenue. (You'll note I stipulated *Melrose Avenue.* On
Hollywood Boulevard he'd go unnoticed every day of
the year.)

The studio has me on a "hold" call. That means that
I won't be working today, but since they're paying me,
anyway, they have the right to tell me that although
I'm not working they have the right to put me on hold.
The inexactness of the foregoing is not capricious. A
word without a definition is a word without a function.
Conversely, since the word "hold" is functionless, it
cannot be defined other than as an example of itself
—*i.e.,* as an example of a word that has no function.
Ergo, being on hold I am functionless and, therefore, in
perfect form to write in this journal today.

I have, as I promised myself last week, decided to
take a busman's holiday and visit the set this morning.

My first view upon entering the soundstage is of Ve
dressed as a female vampire and Janna as a burlesque
queen. They flit in and out of Ilia's quarters dabbing
the noses of Steve Collins and Persis Khambatta. Perhaps if I were working today, if I were in costume myself, I would not find the scene so incongruous, so like
something out of Pirandello. Two sets of pretenders,

after all, but on two different levels. Serious pretenders creating an earnest fiction with the serious aid of whimsical pretenders fashioning a fanciful reality. My initial, somewhat elitist, reaction is that the professional make-believers are reduced in stature by their juxtaposition —worse, their dependency on the amateur ones. If everyone can get into makeup and costume just by willing it, then what is to distinguish us from them? I realize I am making a superficial comparison, but there is another factor to consider, one that nudges me toward a reality warp. The actors are emoting within a fictional framework, but the made-up makeup ladies are functioning within the parameters of factuality. Today is, after all, Halloween. Everyone dresses up on Halloween. In this context, the vampire and the show girl have more credibility than the pretend officers aboard a non-existent spaceship going nowhere. I should have stood in bed.

I wander over to where Mel Traxel sits poring over several dozen photographs lined up on a table. The pics are of all the different mechanical devices—from communicators to sophisticated medical implements— used on the show. My question evokes the logical answer: the photos will be passed on to toy manufacturers. Hopefully they will find among the displayed instruments many they will wish to reproduce for the kiddy trade. I am fully aware of the prodigious market that exists for science-fiction toys and am not surprised by his explanation. In fact, on the heels of it I am struck by a truism which, although not yet recognized by actors operating in this film milieu, soon will be. If you want to be assured your performance doesn't end up on the cutting room floor, make sure you are photographed in close proximity to a marketable gadget. They wouldn't dare cut you out of the movie and sacrifice the bucks that would be lost if the merchandisable doohickey were not seen in the picture.

The ultimate test of movie-moguldom will be to someday create a film in which the hardware plays *all* the roles—starring, supporting, bit, and extra—and every Styrofoam and Plexiglass scrap utilized will be reproduced in miniature for sale at the local five-and-dime.

I leave Mel and spy Robert Wise standing by himself in apparent good spirits. It occurs to me that the mounting problems on this production have not changed the man one whit. The dignity and style with which he comports himself are as they were on the first day of shooting. The crew, to a man, have been unreserved in their respect and praise for our director. Watching him now, I feel compelled to thank him personally on behalf of the entire company. I rush to him in the flush of my enthusiasm and seize his hand. Pumping it a bit frenetically I fear, I babble on my appreciation for some twenty or thirty seconds. When he can at last reclaim his limb, he steps away gingerly as if fearful that a sudden move will cause me to go totally berserk.

He is gone and I'm standing alone, only half my thank you's spent. Gratitudinous interruptus—a whole new area for clinical study.

2:30 p.m.: I've just learned that Franklyn is no longer with the production. *The Onion Field* doesn't start shooting until late November, but rather than involve him in the third act and worry about matching shots if he should suddenly leave in the middle of a sequence, he is excused now. The character he plays in the police story is a killer. Knock 'em dead, Franklyn.

3:45 p.m.: Remember Bert, the production director for Abel and Associates, the guy who told me that "nothing like what *we* are doing (for the effects on the *S.T.* film) has ever been seen before in a motion picture"? Remember how his enthusiasm renewed my confidence in that company's ability to succeed on our behalf? Well, it turns out now that ol' Bert is leaving Abel and Associates. I think someone just cut the tether on my balloon.

I *knew* I should of stood in bed today.

November

SUNDAY, NOVEMBER 5

Opening day of our softball season. Three games are played. "Little House on the Prairie" and "Laverne and Shirley" play evenly in the first, "Happy Days" narrowly wins over Star Trek *in the second, and in the third encounter of the close kind, "Mork and Mindy" edges "Taxi."*

Over 700 people attend the festivities and two huge futuristic (what else?) barrels are full of dollars contributed by the fans for the Muscular Dystrophy Association.

It is particularly enjoyable doing battle with "Happy Days" since they turn out almost their entire cast. Henry Winkler pitches for them. Jimmy Doohan, making his first appearance at our games, starts for us. Bill has made an impassioned plea to Steve (our captain) to let Jimmy pitch on the basis of his experience as a semi-pro back in Canada. It is never quite established just how far "back in Canada" it was, but Mr. Doohan is definitely a bit rusty. He throws twenty-four pitches without getting one called a strike. The bases are loaded and two runs in when I am called upon to relieve. I present all this detail not to embarrass Jimmy (he thought the whole thing funny, anyway), but because what happened next was definitely from the same bag as my bubble-gum-card picture and comic book likeness.

*Let me paint the scene for you: two runs down, the
bases loaded, and nobody out. My first pitch is a strike
and the crowd applauds. The second pitch is also a
strike and the fans are roaring. The third delivery is
hit weakly back to the box, the man is thrown out at
the plate, and now everyone is on his feet in wild approval. Bear in mind that before we started this league
I hadn't played in an organized game of baseball since
the eighth grade. Bear in mind that I'm a devout
Yankee fan and have on more than one occasion put
myself to sleep with fantasies about coming out of the
bullpen to snuff a Dodger rally in the ninth inning of
the last game of the World Series. Bear in mind that I
have made it a cardinal rule to only daydream about
things that could never happen in my life. And so here
I am with 700 people watching, playing against a team
that has played against professionals in Dodger Stadium
with the first out in my pocket. The next batter pops
up and there is pandemonium in the gallery. Two outs
and still no one has scored. As I again stare plateward
my thoughts are centered not on the approaching hit-
ter, but on how absolutely extraordinary this whole situation is. Somewhere beyond the third-base foul line,
tucked away behind the support structure of the stands,
there is a wizard, and alchemist who can transform
wispy daydreams into hard reality. Standing there on
the mound, the ball squeezed in my hand, the crowd
continuing to scream its support, I am experiencing a
first in my life. Four decades on this Earth and there
are still new sensations to feel. I don't have to pretend
to be Sparky Lyle or Rich Gossage; I need only be
Walter Koenig. Eerie, spooky, but what an incredible
high. Even as I wind up for my next pitch I am watching myself on television watching myself pitch. Talk
about dissociation, talk about schizophrenia! I am absolutely two different people named Walter Koenig, and*

for this one focused intense moment the make-believe Walter is as much flesh and blood as the other.

I need hardly put it down, but just for the record, the next batter doubles, and before the smoke has cleared, "Happy Days" leads five to nothing. Ultimately we rally and make the score respectable, but we are losers, nevertheless. Losers, that is, except for me. For a minute and forty-five seconds on this first Sunday in November, Walter Koenig is a genuine American hero.

Another pitcher takes over for our team in the sixth inning and I watch the rest of the game from the stands. Nichelle pinch-hits in our last at-bat, but before she can swing, Henry Winkler leaps from the mound. She meets him halfway and they fall into a mad embrace. Actors being actors, it stands to reason that they had never met before this moment.

One interesting observation: the decibel level of the crowd becomes a perfect audiometer of changing times. When Bill Shatner first arrives, the crowd responds with a healthy roar. Henry Winkler's appearance drives the counter to the far edge. Robin Williams's entrance breaks the sound barrier. It's the Sixties of Kirk, the Seventies of "the Fonz," and, no doubt, the Eighties of Mork. Three decades of mass popularity represented here, and on this sunny day only an attentive ear to distinguish the past from the future.

TUESDAY, NOVEMBER 7

Kirk follows Spock out of the ship and is attacked by a swarm of translucent blobs.

11:00 a.m.: Back to work after a layoff that fell short of its estimated length. Schedule changes, however, have become the norm. It is not possible, quite literally, to predict more than a couple of days in advance which scenes will be shot when.

Whereas our problems earlier stemmed from malfunctioning cameras, special effects complications, human frailty (Persis lost her voice for two days), and uncooperative weather conditions, the current nemesis is a recalcitrant third act. Those involved in approving the script have not yet achieved unanimity. Last night at home I received the rewrites on the last twenty-three pages of the story. In order for them to be delivered to my doorstep in Los Angeles, they had to be first sent by jet to New York for sanction by the studio's chief executives visiting there.

That accomplished, presumably, we are now set to push forward, right? Wrong! Last night's hot-off-the-presses blue pages are today's singing-the-blues news. With the exception of about a half-dozen speeches, the consensus is that the third act still has not come together.

12:30 p.m.: My call was for 11:00 this morning. I know by now that meant I wouldn't be working, if at all, until after lunch. Sure enough, I am dismissed for the midday break while wondering what this midday break is a break from.

The Paramount cafeteria is the one place where I can be assured of no surprises. They always have tuna salad, it always costs $1.80 per ice-cream scoop, and if you sprinkle enough simulated bacon bits and croutons on top of it, it always, gratefully, ends up tasting like simulated bacon bits and croutons.

I do learn something new here today, however. In conversation with a Paramount computer analyst, I discover that the *Star Trek* movie has *already* been sold to television. Once it has its run in movie theaters, it will be aired twice on ABC's small screen to the tune of ten million dollars. If my source is to be believed, this figure represents the most a picture, not yet even completed, has gone for in the television marketplace. He also tells me that the *Star Trek* motion picture does not, in actuality, have any final budget. The twenty-four-million-dollar figure that has been circulating is a departure point, not a final reckoning. As things stand now, the break-even point on the film is projected to be at gross receipts in excess of sixty million dollars. My conversation with him is by no means an official one and I cannot vouch for the authenticity of his figures, but he certainly *sounds* like he knows what he's talking about.

The numbers continue to fly by so fast and furiously that very soon they seem to lose significance. *Saturday Night Fever* has brought in more than sixty million dollars. Paramount is anticipating another two hundred to two hundred forty million by the end of the year from *Grease, Foul Play,* and *Heaven Can Wait.* As I listen to his report, it occurs to me that if *Star Trek* has no finite budget, a debt of thanks is probably owed to John Travolta, Warren Beatty, Goldie Hawn, *et al.*

2:00 p.m.: A great moment in the life of Lieutenant Chekov. Robert Wise gravely approaches. "I had to get Kirk and Spock floating around in space, Decker holed up in engineering with Ilia [unit], Uhura tied to her communications console, and Sulu buttoned to his helm, but I did it and now Chekov has the conn. How about that, George?" [Well, you can't have everything.]

Despite the George-for-Walter error, the Russian's appointment is real—at least as real as it can be considering that we're only making a movie. I am at once put in mind of my reaction the first time I heard I was to rise from ensign to lieutenant for this project. I was absolutely beside myself for about thirty seconds and then terribly embarrassed with myself thereafter for confusing the real person with the alter ego. After all, a promotion in rank in a motion picture doesn't ensure a better role or more money. I mean, I remember seeing war movies where the privates had the leads and the generals were extras! I tell you, this world of *Star Trek* can really get to you after a while.

In any event, sure enough the Russian officer now finds himself in the command chair briefly in charge of the *Enterprise*. We are shooting the six serviceable speeches in the new pages as I push a button and order a rescue team to the side of our blob-besieged battler outside the ship. A curious thing happens to me/Chekov as we watch Kirk's predicament on the viewscreen (post-production optical effect). I find myself, without premeditation, leaning to my left and contemplatively running a finger across my cheek.

After the shot is printed I ask myself: Why that particular gesture? Almost immediately I am blushing as the answer forms itself: it is a gesture I have seen Bill make at the conn time and again. Am I, then, only imitating Bill Shatner in the performance of my performance? I decide to be kinder to myself. Not Koenig and Shatner, but Chekov and Kirk. If Chekov were to unconsciously emulate his Captain, it would be understandable. He undoubtedly looks up to him, feels that he'd like to be like him. What better gauge of the younger man's respect than to pattern himself after his leader. I am enough into my role to do that kind of thing without planning it. Summing up, the gesture is consistent with the character as drawn and valid for the situation. Sounds good to me. Clever devil, this Walter-George-Charlie-Bill-Shatner-stand-in-Koenig guy.

5:40 p.m.: We pull the plug. The rest of the third act is no closer to being solved than it was at the start of the day. As we prepare for home, Kevin informs us that the entire company of actors will convene on Stage Ten at 8:00 tomorrow morning to discuss and hopefully solve the inherent script problems.

While walking toward our cars, George and I comment on the unorthodoxy of such a meeting. We finally conclude that it is actually only one in a series of unconventional occurrences that have dogged this production. "Look at it this way," says George as he slips in behind the wheel, "these constant alterations keep us alert, vibrant, and young." I watch him drive off wondering if Gene Roddenberry and Robert Wise are "looking at it this way."

WEDNESDAY, NOVEMBER 8

Would you believe the blue screen again?

9:00 a.m.: The conference on Stage Ten has been called off. Gene, Harold, Robert Wise, Bill, and Leonard are meeting by themselves. We sit, we drink coffee, we wait.

10:34 a.m.: A decision, unretractable, irrefutable, carved in stone, has been reached: shoot the blue screen. When all else fails we can always shoot past the actors' backs out toward space. In effect, we will be doing the reverse angles of yesterday's work. Up goes the blue screen, on go the lights, out go the new pages.

1:15 p.m.: Robin Williams, everyone's favorite Mork, rides his bicycle over to our soundstage. He explains that he is a big fan of our show and is invited onto the bridge. His wide-eyed admiration notwithstanding, his squeaky-voiced reaction to all the buttons and panels is, "Hmmmm, microwave!"

3:00 p.m.: Undoubtedly the most booorrrring day I've been through on this production. Absolutely nothing to do but watch as the camera sets up in one position, shoots for ten to fifteen seconds past an actor's back, and then moves on to another position. The routine is repeated again and again ad infinitum, ad nauseum.

3:49 p.m.: I find myself greedily listening to a tepid news items being recounted by Anita Terrian, the production assistant. A security guard hired for the picture a few days before had, apparently, been propositioning the women on the show and threatening bodily injury when they demurred. He has already been fired and is long gone, but in my desperate state of ennui I am hoping he will return packing twin 38's and at least shoot out the lights on the blue screen. I decide I will even take a flesh wound in the shoulder if it'll add a little spice to the dreary proceedings.

4:08 p.m.: Thursday promises to be more stimulating. The story conference with all the actors present that was scheduled for today will be held first thing in the morning. I've got some ideas about how the story should be resolved. If the opportunity presents itself on the morrow, I shall definitely step forward.

THURSDAY, NOVEMBER 9

Wherein we learn exactly what V'ger *plans to do to the planet Earth in exactly twenty-nine-point-two minutes.*

7:44 a.m.: There has got to be a conspiracy afoot. I will accept no other explanation. There is a new guard at the gate as I drive up this morning. I have never seen him before and am in the process of rolling down my window to identify myself when he waves me through: "That's all right, I know who you are, *George*."

8:00 a.m.: Bagels, cream cheese, fresh orange juice, and coffee. We repair to Stage Ten for some serious script talk and some serious eating—only Gene, Harold, Bob, Leonard, and Bill aren't there. . . . That's right, they've once again decided to have their meeting in private.

9:15 a.m.: De Forest and I walk the alleys of the Paramount lot throwing ideas at each other and come up with what we are convinced is a very good resolution to the third act. We bump into Richard Kline, the cinematographer, and propose it to him. He likes it despite the fact it would mean reshooting the sickbay scene following Spock's return to the ship. He suggests that we volunteer the concept to the sequestered conferees. De had been invited to join the assembly and now regrets not having done so. All the same, he feels we should wait until the meeting breaks up before offering our suggestions.

10:58 a.m.: The conference is over and we approach Leonard with our proposed changes. Although he acknowledges that the concept has merit, he feels that the problem of reshooting the sickbay scene is overwhelming—this despite the verbatim report of our cinematographer.

De next talks to Bill. At least with him there is no sense of equivocation. He out and out hates the notion. So much for our contribution to the writing of the *Star Trek* movie.

11:15 a.m.: We begin rehearsing the new pages. Uhura has the line: "Captain, the alien has ejected a large object." You don't have to be anally fixated to get a fix on how that might come across in 70-mm Panavision. We all titter like schoolchildren and the line is changed to: "The alien has *released* a large object." Everyone seems convinced that removes the anus onus, but I'm wondering who is kidding whom.

12:05 p.m.: We don't get far enough to record the line on film before it's time for lunch.

I take a shortcut to the cafeteria through Stage Eight and am shocked by the eviscerated condition of the Rec Deck. The walls are gone, the floor is gone, only the structural ribs remain. I am put in mind of those brontosaurus skeletons in the natural history museum. I know what's bothering me. It's more than just the esthetic loss. I am perceiving the disassembly as a metaphor for the *Star Trek* movie itself. The temporal nature of this production and, ultimately, its lack of importance in the greater scope of things becomes painfully clear. The rec hall structure, the result of so much manpower, concentrated energy, and creative input, is being torn down without so much as a backward glance. At best it will be stored away; at worst it will be discarded altogether. The *Star Trek* feature as a whole will eventually share the same fate. This is a world where change runs stride for stride with time. Before too many more clicks of the digital clock, the *Star Trek* movie will have been completed, been released in theaters, been seen on television, and, at best, been stored away somewhere, at worst, been discarded altogether.

On the heels of this thought comes another. The Rec Deck story is more than a metaphor for this motion picture; it is allegorical to human existence itself. Each of us with so much manpower, energy, and creativity to contribute, and before it's half-spent, life is over. It's a damn shame I don't believe in the hereafter.

12:45 p.m.: The bacon bits don't help the tuna scoop this lunchtime.

2:25 p.m.: UHURA: "Captain, the alien has released a large object."

We have taken up where we left off before the noon meal, and so has the laughter. I'm sure it's because of the special juxtaposition of the Earth to the stars and planets at this particular moment that we are responding so boisterously. There is no other way to explain this nuttiness.

Robert Wise attempts to bring order, but he can't hold the company together while he is busy holding his sides. "Next line, next line," he implores through his tears.

SULU: "They've released another one . . . two . . . three more!"

Unbelievably, the laughter swells. The camera crew, the grips, the prop masters; no one is immune. Irrationally, we try to push forward.

McCoy speaks next and for a brief moment De Forest is able to rally the solemn tone the line demands: "They're the same things that hit us."

No one is standing now; no one is able to. Those of us not in chairs are literally rolling on the floor. The tide of laughter rises again. We are definitely in danger of being pulled under. Only Leonard, clinging desperately to his character of Spock, maintains the barest shred of sanity. Alas, even as he fights for control, his generally reliable eyebrow threatens to twitch past his forehead into his hairline.

"Your speech, your speech," gurgles Bill, red-faced and barely coherent through his cachinnation.

"Not on your life," replies Leonard. "I wouldn't touch that line. . . ."

"Please, please!" beg cast and crew alike.

The better self of Leonard loses out to the lesser half of Spock. With a definite human flavor, the Vulcan science officer says, "It's a hundred times more powerful than what hit us."

I should say he *starts* to say. He never quite finishes it. Almost immediately he is helpless like the rest of us. It is as if the little Dutch boy had withdrawn his finger and with it any last hope we might escape the deluge. It is not possible that forty-four responsible, skilled, and respected professionals could react with such unmitigated glee to such obvious and puerile toilet humor, but here we are, every last one of us, about to be flushed away.

3:32 p.m.: When Uhura's line is finally recorded, it is changed to: "A large object has been released by the intruder." It must be okay; we've finally stopped laughing.

FRIDAY, NOVEMBER 10

During which Kirk debates with the Ilia unit as to who is a true life form and who isn't.

8:30 a.m.: The first heavy rain of the shoot. I take Josh with me to the studio this morning. If all the elements are not favorable on this wet and cold day, at least the one my son is in must be. He's having a ball. He loves being here; he'd love to be an actor. How do I tell him that for every *Star Trek* there are a dozen "Charlie's Angels," and for every "Charlie's Angels" there are

5,000 actors in Hollywood who can't get a television job of any kind?

9:55 a.m.: A couple of new new white pages have come down, and with the changes acknowledged, the company continues to shoot the sequence begun yesterday.

No one is prepared to say I won't work today, but the angle they're shooting from would suggest that my cubbyhole is not in the day's plans. With that thought in mind I choose not to dress. Those that do are issued booties to protect the pant-shoe uniform combination from the rain. It's a very reasonable safeguard. I've just been told that to custom-build the shoes into the pants cost five hundred dollars a pair.

10:25 a.m.: My first blow-up, and at, of all people, Elaina, our pregnant security guard. I should be ashamed of myself. It happens when she informs me that there would be no room on the soundstage for the guests I have invited for the afternoon. I pull rank and call the front office demanding satisfaction. Astonishingly, even here I am given no assurances.

12:00 p.m.: I begin the rest of the morning fretting and fuming over the inequities of this situation. From there it is a short steamroll into a diatribe about the inequity of all existence. Needless to say, by noon my mood is darker than the drenching skies.

2:09 p.m.: This morning's tirade notwithstanding, my friends have to wait in my dressing room for forty minutes before being allowed onto the set.

Soundstage Nine is still the hardest ticket in town. It seems as if everybody in the world would like to visit the *Enterprise*. I have received requests to come aboard from Yugoslavia, from Italy, from Japan, from Germany (more like a demand), from Iceland, and from New Jersey.

The letter from New Jersey was particularly unique. The young woman threatened to "get me" if I didn't send her an airplane ticket. It was obviously a case of the cranks and I quickly dispatched the missive to the wastepaper basket. All the same, sending it as she did by special delivery and signing her name with the blood from her finger does tend to make one pause.

2:20 p.m.: The new, new, *new* white pages have come down. There is a new coding system on the rewrites. In addition to the day and the month of the year, the top margin on each page includes the time of the day for each draft and the initials of the author responsible. Since not every speech on every page is revised by the alternating writers, more than one set of initials frequently borders the succeeding versions. Thus, across the top of the latest edition the nomenclature is: HL— 11/9/78; GR—11/10/78; HL—11/10/78, 2:00 P.M.; to distinguish it from this morning's rewrites, which read: HL—11/9/78; GR—11/10/78, 9:30 A.M. I'm not sure whether this procedure is used simply to identify the most current collaborative effort or whether it is some kind of rule imposed by the Screen Writers Guild for the purpose of establishing writing credits, but either way it has us giggling.

You'd probably had to have been here, but John Black, the key grip, gets a big laugh when he throws down the 2:00 P.M. edition in mock disgust and says he refuses to work until he gets the *blue* rewrites.

4:39 p.m.: The 4:00 P.M. edition of the revised version of the altered pages of the changed script is now in our hands. I no longer insert these wet-inked copies into my script binder. As sure as there are stars in the solid arch, these sheets shall beget progeny.

5:37 p.m.: As I had suspected might happen, they have not gotten to me today. "First thing Monday morning," I am told. I step out into the night air and discover the rain has stopped. The sky seems to be clearing. It's a good omen. I feel better already. First thing Monday morning Chekov will be working, and first thing Monday morning Walter will apologize to Elaina.

"Wait a minute, Walter," says Kevin, coming up behind me. "You forgot these."

Would you believe the 5:45 P.M. rendering, of the 4:00 version of the 2:00 edition of the . . . ? Well, you get the idea.

SUNDAY, NOVEMBER 12

10:00 a.m.: It rained all day yesterday, but as if by divine intervention the clouds are gone and the sun is out for our softball game against "The Rockford Files." The field is muddy so a makeshift diamond is paced off in an adjoining grassy area. Due to the ground conditions, the game is sanctioned an exhibition rather than a league competition. Sounds like big-time stuff. Amazing how seriously weekend athletes will take themselves with just a little encouragement.

"Rockford" is shot at Universal, not Paramount, but having gotten wind of our enterprise, they've asked to be included. As an unsolicited party to the festivities, you'd think they'd act with a bit more decorum. Jim Garner is on the mound for them, and from the very first pitch he is haranguing the umpire. Despite his unabating baiting, his maverick throws are being called accurately by the man behind the plate. To give Garner his due, each barb is humorously wrought and it's not possible to get too upset with him.

All the same, I take considerable satisfaction when, in the bottom of the first inning, he hits my first pitch of the game weakly back at me. Realizing the futility of running the grounder out on a bum leg, he starts back toward his bench. I am still smugly glowing over his ineffectiveness when I cock my arm to throw the ball to the first-baseman. A moment later I am in a state of total panic as I realize the fielder is looking at me in utter stupefaction and making no effort to catch the toss. Only after the film star has returned to the basepaths and is hobbling toward first does it occur to me that something is definitely wrong and I am probably to blame for it. A moment later as the world comes back into focus, the "probably" is replaced by absolute certainty. Somehow, in flexing my elbow for the throw, I have inexplicably lost my grip on the sphere and actually released it behind my ear, dribbling it in the general direction of third base. Only in those dreams where I can't find my clothes and am forced to serve chipped beef and Melba toast in the raw to a luncheon of the Women's Presbyterian Society have I ever suffered such acute embarrassment. Here are all these guys performing in such earnest jockdom, and here am I performing like my five-year-old daughter. Gads!

As the game progresses we surge ahead, then fall behind, then fall further behind. The "Rockford" rascals are playing rogue softball. Their third-baseman misses a tag on me sliding in and threatens to atone for his fielding collapse by collapsing my duodendum. I laugh (a bit nervously) and attempt a discourse on the impropriety of physical abuse. There is, however, blood in his eye and spittle between his teeth, and very quickly I abandon the effort.

Needless to say, it is a source of enormous satisfaction that we score four runs in the last inning and beat them nine to eight.

MONDAY, NOVEMBER 13

Today we play cat and mouse with V'ger. Kirk orders the crew to clear the bridge in an attempt to bluff the adversary.

9:11 a.m.: The first shots of the day are of Chekov. On Friday it was again a case of not being able to position the camera to incorporate the weaponry console in the master shot. Since my character does have lines in the sequence, he cannot very well be excluded completely. Now, with all the medium and tight shots that evolve from the master in the can and out of the way, they are able to break down the previous setup and begin a new one.

The new perspective parallels the Russian's profile, but from a position below him on the lower deck of the bridge. The prior line had been Kirk's, so that when Chekov speaks it is to the Captain he turns. However, this is a new setup from a new angle, and if I were to look to the conn where Kirk was actually sitting it would appear as if I were not looking at him at all. The frame of reference has changed from the preceding shot of the Captain and I must, therefore, compensate by looking almost directly above the camera rather than thirty degrees to my right, where the command chair is really positioned. Thus, when I announce that Earth's defense systems have just been rendered inoperative, I am really saying it to a metal light pole about two inches in diameter. I've heard of characters with a lean and hungry look, and Bill has done admirably well in keeping his weight down, but this . . .

9:48 a.m.: Remember earlier when I mentioned picking up shots from other sequences when the camera position lends itself to doing so? This is such a case. Robert Wise has decided to use this setup to record some Chekov action for a scene not yet rehearsed with the other actors. The danger in this stems from our myriad script alterations and the possibility that my character's lines may have been changed by the time the rest of the scene goes before the camera. We shall see.

11:05 a.m.: It is raining, mirky, and very cold, and the power is out in the dressing rooms. I am, therefore, writing this by the light in my eyes and the heat of my passion. Unfortunately, I've just learned that the call sheet has George, Nichelle, and me finishing in the picture on Thursday. Consequently, I am having a dickens of a time seeing what it is my numb fingers are scribbling.

1:30 p.m.: The major event of the early afternoon is the drop of blue cheese dressing I have accidentally spilled on my pant-shoe during lunch. (I was supposed to take off my costume at the noon break and didn't.) I inform Wardrobe of my carelessness and it is immediately treated like a major catastrophe. I half-expect the Red Cross with sirens wailing to come rolling onto the soundstage. You cannot believe the number of people who are suddenly mobilized to confront this act of sabotage. People rushing to find my second pair of pants, people rushing to find out when I will be needed

on camera, people rushing to find a cleaning solution—
you'd have sworn that seven sticks of dynamite and a
clock had been wired together somewhere on Stage
Nine. I realize that the pant-shoes cost five hundred
dollars, but it's only one eensy-weensy stain. Gosh, if
I can get this much action out of a small glob of dressing, think what I could do if I poured the entire tuna
salad over me! Better yet, think of the favor I'd be
doing my stomach!!

2:48 p.m.: A story conference involving all the actors
has at last been called. It turns out to be something less
than an in-depth discussion of character and plot. Actually, with all the script changes being made, we spend
the time trying to figure out if everyone has the most
current revised versions: "Mine says: HL—11/13/78."
"Mine says: HL—11/10/78; GR—11/10/78; HL—
11/10/78." "Is that 2:00 or 4:00?" "Mine says 5:45."
"It should read: *Revised* HL—11/13/78." "Mine says
re-revised." "On 11/10 or 11/13?" "Is the 5:45 GR
or HL . . . ?"

. . . and the door mouse said to Alice, "Have a cup
of tea?"

3:11 p.m.: We begin rehearsing the new sequence in
which the Captain calls for the bridge to be evacuated.
It will again be a master shot that doesn't include my
alcove. However, my part in this action was recorded
this morning when our director chose to film my speech
in advance of the rest of the scene.

I am now told by Bonnie that my lines spoken
earlier have now been changed (I should go into the
seer business) and that the words as delivered for
the camera are no longer viable. Whether or not they
will reshoot is moot, but, she informs, when I say them

off-camera in this master setup, I should use the corrected phrasing.

. . . to which Alice politely replied . . .

4:44 p.m.: There are a couple of people on the set doing interviews for a national newspaper syndicate. I talk and talk and talk into a tape recorder answering question after question about Chekov—his life, his goals, his relationships. Partly because I've responded to these questions a hundred times before and partly because there isn't one query among the host into the life and times of Walter Koenig, I am growing very weary. I am surreptitiously signaling to Suzanne Gordon of the publicity department to get me out of this when my male interviewer leans over and whispers one last question in my ear: "Is it true that Chekov intends to become the next great stud of the universe?" I can't quite believe what I've heard. I look to see if he's joking. He is not. He appears so serious, in fact, that I'm put in mind of that unfortunate young woman who confessed to me at a convention that she had a completely satisfying fantasy life with Mr. Spock. It seems clear to me now why this fellow asked only about my character and not me. It would appear that for him Pavel is a lot more substantive than is Walter. I think I'm about to have an identity crisis.

5:29 p.m.: We chew the scenery a bit more but do not immortalize the mastication. Tomorrow we'll do it all again for the magic eye.

6:45 p.m.: At home. Two invitations have come in the mail. One is for lunch at the home of Robert and Millicent Wise on the 26th of November, and the other is for a party hosted by Bill and Leonard at the Los Angeles Rams football game on December 17. I guess

Leonard offered to divide the sponsorship. They're calling it a wrap party. Indeed, the days are dwindling
down to a precious few.

TUESDAY, NOVEMBER 14

We evacuate the bridge, V'ger *calls the bluff, and Earth
is still in a* lot *of trouble.*

10:15 a.m.: Bill asks Mr. Wise if we can rehearse and
shoot the events leading up to the evacuation and the
evacuation itself in toto. I skim the script and discover
he is talking about almost five full pages. That's a big
chunk under any circumstances, but doubly ambitious
when you consider it involves fourteen people in motion
with seven of them having lines.

Bill feels we can all get a better feeling for the sense
and intensity of what we are doing if we play the whole
thing uninterrupted in the master setup. There is obvious merit in the suggestion. On the other hand, it is
also true that after we finish the master we will shoot
the same sequence again and again in bits and pieces
from new angles and sizes. These different setups will
be intercut into the original shot so that in the final
edited version relatively little of the master will remain
in the movie.

The question, then, before the board is: Do we spend
the many hours it will require to get the five pages in
one take toward the goal of nuance and shading in the
actors' performances but at the sacrifice of time, money,
and our shooting schedule?

Our director, consistently accommodating to the
cause of art, accedes to Bill's request.

11:43 a.m.: We break for lunch still in rehearsal, still trying to solve the problems of staging this complicated piece of business.

12:43 p.m.: I join Iva and the two Ralphs at Oblath's, a convenient close-by restaurant. When the checks come, automatically and in unison—almost like a routine, in fact—they tear off and pocket the stubs. What with agents' commissions, state and federal taxes, a contribution to the actors' fund, etc., it is not unusual for the struggling thespian to net as little as forty-five percent of his weekly salary. With this in mind, every statistical scrap that can substantiate a business expense is horded with the hope of exacting a refund from the I.R.S. at tax time. "An actor's lot is not an easy one," to paraphrase Gilbert and Sullivan.

There is some validity in the bipolar view that performers are "either—or." There are the handful that have income in seven figures and the seventy-five percent who earn less than three thousand dollars a year from their chosen profession. It hardly seems fair, and, of course, it isn't. There is as much talent at the bottom of the economic pyramid as there is at the top. What drives the vast majority to stick with it? The brass ring? A need that transcends the comfort of a full stomach? Whatever. Success or failure, there is nobility in the pursuit and I applaud my luncheon companions and all the other actors who scrimp and save and sacrifice and find a way to hang in there.

2:38 p.m.: We have been back rehearsing the evacuation sequence for about an hour and are now close to rolling the camera. We take a short break while last-minute preparations are made and Jeff Katzenberg, Paramount's vice-president in charge of this production, steps forward. I have noticed the last few times he's visited that he seems less preoccupied, more outgoing, considerably warmer. I'm sure his deportment is at least partly attributable to the edited sequences that the studio brass has been viewing.

I'm rather intrigued by this Katzenberg fellow. He is extremely young, no more than thirty or thirty-one, looks twenty-five, and carries enormous responsibility as studio overseer of this film and several others shooting around the globe. How has he come so far so fast?

Who am I kidding? I know the answer. This is truly a world for the very young, and as the years advance around my temples I am more and more cognizant that nowhere is this concept more glorified than in the film business.

I am put in mind of *Logan's Run*. Specifically, as it relates to the actor's and, even more specifically, to the actress's plight in this town. Youth is so revered that, quite literally, once past twenty-three or twenty-four, the attractive young performer is considered beyond his/her peak in terms of physical appeal. Of course, there are exceptions, but there are also a hell of a lot of buses headed in the other direction carrying faces which by other standards would still be considered new and fresh.

Filmic heros have long functioned as the idealized self of the public. No wonder, then, in our striving we would try to imitate art. If the people who have the most exciting adventures, the most heroic encounters, the most marvelous romances, and the best sex are under thirty, then in order to achieve the optimum results behind the camera we must hire those who must closely resemble the fantasy images up there on the screen.

This obviously isn't an indictment of Jeff Katzenberg. The bottom line is still performance. If he wasn't doing the job, he wouldn't be here. I just wonder if he would have gotten the chance so quickly if our society, by way of its media, was not so youthfully oriented.

I am roused from my musings as he now approaches and confirms that he is pleased with the edited footage he has seen. He also talks about all of us getting together after the picture is done to discuss a promotion campaign that will apparently include the "convention type of thing."

5:25 p.m.: At 2:45 we stopped rehearsing the evacuation scene and began shooting it. Two hours and forty minutes later we've finally gotten one in the can that satisfies all parties. The sequence runs 320 film feet, which translates (at ninety feet per minute) as three minutes and fifty seconds of film time. There was a plethora of problems along the way: actors forgetting lines, K-10s that weren't lit, actors forgetting lines, shaky camera moves, actors forgetting lines. . . .

Take Thirteen, which would only have *tied* the record for the most futile attempts at a serviceable print, was perfect, except that on re-examining the camera lens a hair was discovered across the aperture. We excede the former record by two before everything finally comes together on Take Fifteen.

6:11 p.m.: There is just time to start breaking down the long master and shoot a three-shot of some of the same action before it's time to call it a night.

On Monday the weekly call sheet had it that Thursday would be my last day. Even with anticipated changes there are at least a dozen pages left to do on the bridge. We begin taking bets as to whether we'll be here through Thanksgiving.

WEDNESDAY, NOVEMBER 15

The longest exit in the history of the theater: we are still evacuating the bridge.

7:45 a.m.: Makeup room. Bill tells a story about an aggressive executive whose punch-in-the-arm morning salutation is forty percent warmth and sixty percent hostility. In the course of demonstrating the man's delivery, he delivers an uppercut to an imaginary subject, somehow misses the thin air, and lands a painful blow to his own nose. I wouldn't have believed it if I hadn't seen it. Besides being incredibly funny, it is a devastating argument against going to work and trying to function at such an early hour.

8:30 a.m.: Yesterday's dailies were viewed at seven this morning. The consensus is that the long and difficult master shot was well worth the time and care. Richard Kline has consistently come up with exciting and innovative footage, and here again he has apparently topped himself. It is little wonder he is considered among the best cinematographers in the business. It is also little wonder that he and Robert Wise have worked together before. They complement each other beautifully. Richard is a gentleman in every sense of the word. You know the way it is with some people—there is a special thing about them that makes you feel good by their just saying hello. He was the cinematographer on the "Mr. Novak" shows I did way back in 1964 and 1965. I liked him then. His rise to the top has not dimmed my view one whit.

9:09 a.m.: The first setup of the morning is a group composition. It is the last sequence in the evacuation.

Uhura, Sulu, and Chekov are already in one elevator, with Spock, McCoy, Decker, and Kirk about to join them. It is at this point that *V'ger,* through the Ilia unit, begins negotiating with the Captain. While this is going on we remain in the elevator. The close quarters are stuffy enough, but with the addition of "dinks," "babies," and "juniors," the elevator is fast becoming a small inferno. There are the usual delays in starting. We are nevertheless asked to remain at our post. The lights are hot and we are tired. Nichelle decides to take off her shoes and do the scene standing on an "apple box." (I am surprised to see that she has a pair of uniform slacks that are separate from the shoes.)

Standing on the box, she is several inches taller than she was before, and George and I beside her are now dwarfed by the added stature. There's no point in our getting on the box, too, since the shoes we are wearing would then swing the difference in height disproportionately in our favor. Rather than complain and force her back into her tight-fitting shoes, we try a different adjustment on our positioning. George stands in front of her with his toes on the floor and his heels raised to the edge of the box. I stand behind her on the box but with my heels hanging off the back end. My height over her is in this way only increased by the thickness of my soles. The problem is that I'm having difficulty maintaining my balance with only half a foot for support.

Nobody on the other side of the camera realizes that we are using the box because the other actors are standing in front of the elevator entrance blocking the lower half of our bodies. They assume that we are all standing flatfooted on the elevator floor. The point of all this is that I am cautioned repeatedly to stop swaying. I am torn between confessing the situation and jeopardizing Nichelle's arches or gutting it out. I opt for the latter. The heat and my precarious perch prove to be too much. Right in the middle of an otherwise excellent take I go toppling backward. There is considerable screaming and pulling of hair. No one can understand how a person could fall off a flat surface. I'm in it this deep already; I decide to let them keep wondering.

12:35 p.m.: The rest of the morning is spent shooting pieces of yesterday's master. With some time to kill I take advantage of an invitation extended by Robin Williams to watch a "Mork and Mindy" rehearsal. His set is at the other end of the lot. I am checking the numbers on the buildings trying to locate his when I do a double take. I am standing directly in front of the *old* "Star Trek" soundstage, the one where we used to shoot the television series a decade ago. I find myself rooted. I stare up at the building and can't turn away. I don't know what show shoots there now, and I don't want to know. I am being bombarded by memory. For a moment I am absolutely sure that if I open these heavy metal doors I will step into the past. Everything will be as it was. What an eerie feeling and how curious that the only two moments of strong *déjà vu* I have experienced on this new production should occur on the first day of the shoot and now on what is close to the last.

I finally tear myself away and locate "Mork and Mindy." It is a joy to watch Robin work. He is so free and spontaneous. If "Star Trek" ever comes back as a series, Mork or some relative of his will have to make an appearance on the show.

3:00 p.m.: Harold Livingston is co-author with Gene of the *Star Trek* screenplay. He was off the project for a while but has returned to do a great deal of the rewriting. Harold has been coming by more and more frequently lately, sometimes hourly, shuffling hot-off-the-mimeo revisions. This is one such time. Into a corner he goes with Bill and Leonard. Semicolons and exclamation points are discussed with the gravity of a Yalta Conference. Out goes the old-new version, in goes the new-new version of the still wet-inked-behind-the-already-dog-eared rewrites.

5:35 p.m.: It's been another one of *those* afternoons. They have continued to shoot different setups of the master completed yesterday. I have not been called, but not excused, either, and so have spent the time in my dressing room writing in this journal.

Kevin has just now come by to release me. There is icing on his chin and I learn that I missed a birthday celebration for Richard Kline a short while before. There was, of course, the obligatory cake with the ubiquitous *Enterprise* adorning it. I am wondering if the obligatory and ubiquitous publicity department, with cameras snapping, snapping, snapping, was there, too.

THURSDAY, NOVEMBER 16

The time for the Earth's destruction is drawing near. The countdown has begun.

8:45 a.m.: The first setup of the morning is in close on Chekov at his console. The one good thing about being stuck away in a corner of the bridge is that when they do use the Russian in the film it will be primarily in single shots. Because I am infrequently used in a master, there is no choice but to go to these individual angles to include me in the action.

9:25 a.m.: It turns out that they are reshooting the unusable Chekov speech filmed on Monday. The new words are: "They reach final position in twenty-seven minutes mark." The new words are also: "They reach final position in twenty-four minutes mark." In addition, the new words are: "They reach final position in twenty-two minutes mark." There is a good reason for the alternative lines. Due to the many script changes, no one yet knows how long the rest of the action will run. At the same time, the time factor in the Russian's speech is the beginning of a countdown that will be closely watched by the *Enterprise* crew. The alternate lines are, therefore, a protection against the ultimate length of the story. In other words, should we have only recorded Chekov's "twenty-seven minutes" line and the rest of the film ran considerably less than that, it would be apparent to the audience that we were not using story time to movie time as literally as was our intention.

All of this, however, does not explain my consternation after delivering the first of the choices for the camera. That state is induced after Robert Wise asks Tom Overton, the sound mixer, if he could understand the second half of my Russian-accented speech. The rejoinder from Tom is that he couldn't understand the *first* half. The laughter the remark evokes is bad enough, but is nothing compared to the dismay I feel when he adds that he is convinced I am now speaking with a different dialect altogether.

The felony is compounded when our new hairdresser —a nice woman with maternal instincts but totally unfamiliar with Star Trek—rushes up to me. As she smoothes the back of my hair, she whispers in my ear that I shouldn't let these people bother me. "What you're doing is fine," she says. And then she adds, "It sounds just as Mexican as it did before."

12:00 p.m.: Whatever the accent has finally turned out to be, I am finished speaking it by ten after ten. The next hour and forty-six minutes is spent in discussion with other bridge members. The new call sheet has the bridge personnel finishing on Friday. We were all sure we'd go into next week, but if the tag for the story (the scene following the climax) comes down soon and is a page or less, it is quite possible we will all have been wrong. It is a certainty, we decide, that we will finish today the bridge sequences on hand. The twelve pages that were still to be done as of Tuesday afternoon have gone quicker than anticipated. Finishing completely on Friday, therefore, is not out of the question.

Not out of the question, that is, until four minutes before twelve, when we are handed an entirely new bridge scene that runs *eight* pages long. The tag, by the way, is still in the typewriter.

We are now told that our presence is requested on Stage Ten for a rehearsal of the new pages.

1:00 p.m.: In addition to the cast and our director, Harold and Jon Povill are also present. The conversation is lively and stimulating. There always has to be a certain amount of self-serving going on when actors are contributing to a discussion of their character's lines, but in this case it is almost negligible.

I am impressed by the lucidity with which ideas are being proposed and the very positive suggestions that are being made. Bill, in particular, has an awesome grasp of dramatic structure and character integrity. I have always thought of him as simply an actor, one whose intelligence and interests are focused narrowly in his profession, and I have been dead wrong. In the fifteen weeks on this picture, I have learned more about him than I did in the two years on the series. I have discovered that he possesses a keen sense of perception and a broad expanse of knowledge beyond the motion picture arena.

The discussion now underway concerns the exactness of the dialogue in satisfying the character needs of *V'ger,* Spock, and Decker. We infer from the written word that *V'ger* lacks something to make it whole and that Decker believes that by learning what this missing element is he will fill the void in his own life. Furthermore, Spock, having found through his contact with *V'ger* his own answers, understands the nature of *V'ger*'s quest and is thus able to counsel Decker. It is good story construction to have the needs of the various characters interdependent, and no one takes issue with the overall concept. Back and forth they go, however, shaping the words to make the intentions as clear as possible.

Harold has been over this ground a hundred times and is confident that the dialogue as written satisfies the scene's requirements. There is evidence of fatigue about him now, but he will not be dissuaded. He stands gavel to gavel with the actors and director as ideas are examined, re-examined, cross-examined. It is altogether perhaps five speeches, twenty lines, that are before the bar, but it is more than an hour before a verdict is reached. As is often the case when perceptive minds interact, the result achieved is better than the parts.

I come away feeling we are now very close to making the picture as strong at the end as it is in the beginning and middle.

2:30 p.m.: We are now shooting the first part of the new eight-page scene. The opening shot is a dolly move and for the first time the camera is navigated along tracks. The tracks are used to give the camera its smoothest ride around the turns of the circular bridge.

The shot is designed to start at Chekov's console as he reads out pertinent information and then truck toward other stations as the various crew members add to the data. Chekov's speech again refers to the time element and so must again be shot three times: "Twenty-five minutes to device activation"; "Twenty-two minutes to device activation"; "Eighteen minutes to device activation." Considering that we are tempting fate by triplicating the delicate dolly move, we manage to get the shot in relatively few takes.

3:17 p.m.: I intercept what appears at first glance to be an official communiqué, from Gene Roddenberry to Robert Wise: "Bob, any chance we could intercut footage here from your *I Want to Live* flick at this story point and thus wrap the bridge shooting quicker?" An investigation reveals that this missive is just one in a long line of nutty notes between Billy Van Zandt, our resident alien, and Doug Wise, the second assistant director. I also learn that the other bridge personnel, Iva and the two Ralphs, having contributed to these nonsense memos from time to time, are also in on the gag.

I find this interesting because it points up to me that as close an eye as I have tried to keep on things, there are probably a host of happenings concerning this project that have taken place without my knowledge. Susan Sackett will be doing a book on the making of the movie. It will obviously be from the executive point of view. I'm sure it will cover many of the areas, principally those behind closed doors, that I have not been exposed to. I look forward to reading it.

4:11 p.m.: Jon Povill comes by. Remember when they cut out a seven-page scene to bring the playing time down to two hours and ten minutes? Well, after all the rewrites, GR, HL, 2:00 P.M., 4:30 P.M., 5:45 P.M., the running time for the script, Jon tells me, is now just under three hours.

Since the plan is still to release the film at 130 minutes, there will at least be plenty of "never-before-seen" footage for the television airings.

FRIDAY, NOVEMBER 17

Kirk orders Scotty to prepare to execute Starfleet order two-zero-zero-five.

9:33 a.m.: They have started shooting the second half of the new pages. It is now evident we will not finish the bridge sequences until Tuesday or Wednesday of next week. Early on, when our progress was even slower, we would joke that the bridge sequences might not finish before Thanksgiving. Next Thursday is Thanksgiving. Apparently we knew something we didn't know.

1:00 p.m.: George and I go to lunch at Oblath's. I suggest that the two of us host some kind of party for cast and crew on our last day. He's immediately enthusiastic and we draw up plans for a Greek dinner party for next Wednesday.

2:11 p.m.: After discovering that we can't get a take-out Greek dinner for sixty people, we decide on a Hungarian buffet for seventy-five.

2:24 p.m.: When that proves economically unfeasible, we settle on a Chinese lunch for one hundred.

3:56 p.m.: I have not yet worked today and it is evident that I shall not be called upon the rest of the afternoon. I spend the time completing a script I've been given to read by one of the crew guys. It's his first effort and it shows. I applaud his desire and ambition to broaden his vistas, but this attempt is woefully inadequate.

I feel compelled to be honest with him and tactfully point out the weakness in his work. As I have anticipated, he is badly brought down, but, unexpectedly, he also expresses enormous gratitude for my being so straightforward with him. He tell me that most of his associates would have told him it was great regardless of what they thought. He repeats several times that I am a true friend for not misleading him.

I am absolutely floored by his words. What sort of business is this we operate in? Oscar Levant said that beneath the tinsel of Hollywood is the real tinsel. Is phonydom so rampant in this town that an expression of painful candor is deemed an act of kindness?

5:20 p.m.: We are handed the call sheets for next week. According to the schedule, it's a definite maybe we will finish the bridge stuff on Monday . . . or Tuesday . . . or Wednesday . . . or . . .

Oh, yes, we are also given the yellow and pink revisions for scenes 335 through 349 on pages 114 through 119A. Unfortunately, these scenes are already in the can. We finished filming them last Tuesday.

SUNDAY, NOVEMBER 19

Our softball game is with "Taxi." Bill opens in short center, Steve in left field, George catches, and I'm pitching.

I've already had one experience feeling what it was like being in the shoes of a major-league pitcher when we played "Happy Days." I now have my second—at least the shoes of a major-league pitcher who is on his way back to the minors. In the second inning I give up back-to-back home runs to Judd Hirsch and Tony Danza. Undoubtedly, two of the most prodigious clouts in the history of softball.

Bill doubles twice, Steve makes several circus catches in left field, and George lines a single over second. Dan Maltese (set designer) and Kris Gregg (miniature maker) are our surest fielders at third and short and our best hitters. Danny hits two home runs, Chris one, and despite the pitching lapse, we win, 12 to 9.

That's two victories in a row. Remember when they used to say "Break up the Yankees!"? I think we've got a dynasty going here.

MONDAY, NOVEMBER 20

V'ger has us in a tractor beam. We are being pulled from one chamber into another, deeper and deeper inside the vessel. In the distance there is an "island" and on the island some kind of solid matter. It appears that it is from there that V'ger functions.

9:09 a.m.: Once again, Chekov is the first shot of the morning. "Keptin, en oxyajin grravity ahnvwelop iss formink ahutside de *Ainterrpriiss!*" Such intensity, such involvement! Again and again I repeat the words, each time improving on perfection. At last the ultimate performance. It can't be done any better: not by Brando, not by Olivier, not by Akim Tamiroff. I raise out of my chair flushed with triumph. Alas, the celebration is short-lived. I now discover that Chekov's speech, rich in tone and in information vital to ship, compatriots, and plant, has been delivered (and recorded forever on celluloid) with his fly open.

11:35 a.m.: It is a single on Mr. Spock. He stands immobile, barely breathing. "The plan must be implemented immediately, Spock," is Bill's off-camera line. Only, for some inexplicable reason, the words come out, "The device must be . . . done immediately, Spock." Of course, it doesn't make any sense. Of course, it sounds ridiculous delivered as it is by the very earnest Captain, but it is an off-camera line and will not be heard in the film. So, then, what of Mr. Nimoy? Will he let the absurdity of the speech faze him? Will he lose his concentration? Damn right! Leonard leans on the bridge railing for support. Tears roll down his cheeks. He may never stop laughing.

1:48 p.m.: Nichelle says she would like to co-host the party with George and me. We are happy to oblige.

3:00 p.m.: Kirk, Spock, McCoy, Decker, and the Ilia unit leave the *Enterprise* for the island site within *V'ger* chamber. As with the earlier scene when Spock left the ship and Kirk followed, this new space-walk episode will be filmed in the succeeding weeks on new sets being erected on Stages Seventeen, Six, and Fifteen. For now, however, there is nothing more to shoot. The tag has not yet come down and we are pretty much done with the last of the eight new pages. So, naturally, we do what we always do when there is nothing else to do: we do the blue screen.

I am not released even though it is certain that the camera cannot be positioned to shoot past me out into space. I do not mind. There is so little time left on the production that I'm not anxious to remove myself from the proceedings even as a non-participant. I do not feel I have savored all that there is to savor. Surely, there are experiences I have not yet had, opportunities to feel and to learn that I have not yet recognized. I am like the consumer whose impulse is to ravage the supermarket in anticipation of a food shortage. I am suddenly consumed by the urge to stockpile, to horde, to take with me beyond the gates of Paramount enough memories to last through a famine of intense feeling, through all of the mundanity that life is mostly about.

And then I'm introduced to a little boy of seven. He is visiting the *Star Trek* set. It is very nearly his last wish. He will never see the *Star Trek* movie. He will most likely not see the new year. A doctor holds his hand as he waves good-bye to us. As I watch him go, the need to glut myself begins to fade. The mundanity that life is mostly about is not a thing to be dismissed so casually.

TUESDAY, NOVEMBER 22

The tag, at last.

6:27 a.m.: I have some time this morning before I'm due at the studio. I pick up the script and again read through the climactic scene at the island site. Wow! I know I am viscerally oriented and tend to get carried away by small events, but in this case I'm convinced the excitement I feel is proportionate to the concepts on the printed page. One of the indictments of science-fiction movies is that they can never transcribe the imagination embodied in the world of words to the world of the cinema. Well, Gene and Harold have obviously decided that they would not let that antiquated concept inhibit their scenario. There are no apologies here. This sequence—like the wormhole, like the *V'ger* cloud, like a half-dozen other extraordinary episodes in the picture—is described with a lushness that takes the breath away. Here I am, four months after beginning on this project, a day from finishing in it, and I'm getting excited all over again. Wow!

7:47 a.m.: The tag is handed me as I sit down in the makeup chair. Across from me Leonard is being administered to by Fred Phillips. De is close by. They ask my reaction to the pages I have just now finished reading. Their concern is that the two-page tag is too solemn, that it doesn't have the moment of lightness expected in a *Star Trek* story ending. Leonard proposes an acerbic exchange between Spock and McCoy that is funny and consistent with their relationship. My reaction, however, is tempered by my concern that it shifts focus away from what the story is really about. Leonard's reaction to my reaction is a studious "Hmmmm, interesting." And then: "Who the hell asked you, anyway?!" I sense he will return to the drawing board.

9:52 a.m.: Back on the soundstage. They are again shooting blue screen. I ask Danny McCauley how things are going. His eyes roll heavenward. It's not a good sign; it's another bleak, cold day and we are being pelted by a heavy rain.

Billy Van Zandt, our resident alien, has been nicknamed "the geek." Undoubtedly, it is because in his elaborate alien head appliance he looks like he might eat live animals. In any event, the following conversation has just taken place outside the soundstage within earshot of a Paramount employee unfamiliar with the workings of the *Star Trek* project:

RALPH BYERS: Has the geek gotten into head yet?

IVA LANE: No, they're still on the other side [of the bridge].

RALPH BYERS: Doing P.O.V.'s?

IVA LANE: Of blue.

RALPH BYERS: When do we tag?

IVI LANE: [facetiously]: After the 2:10 pinks, the 4:11 blues, and the 5:36 yellows.

The uninitiated employee left shaking his head in bewilderment. It seems that after nearly sixteen weeks aboard this movie we have begun to develop a subculture replete with a language all our own.

12:00 p.m.: It's lunchtime again. I sit at a table with Barbara Minster, our hairdresser. As we start winding down the production more and more, the conversation turns to the finished product. It is no different here. Her bubbling enthusiasm is noteworthy. Barbara never watched "Star Trek" when it was a television series and was not particularly impressed by being appointed to the movie production. During the months she has been with us, however, she has undergone a change. Even though she sees the project every day, shorn of its fantasy, in all its gear-grinding sputtering progress, the mystique of Star Trek has somehow taken hold of her. She has become a FAN. The conversion was completed on the day of the Rec Deck sequence. There she was, dressed as a crew member, applauding along with the 300 other extras when Captain Kirk made his entrance. A born-again Trekkie. A truly uplifting concept.

2:51 p.m.: Now that I am aware of Billy's notes to Doug, I seek out a reading of today's memo. Apparently there are many among the crew who look forward to these missives. Dennis Jones, the sound-boom man, is one. He has asked Tom Overton, the sound mixer, to let him know when the latest flash comes off the wires in Billy's head. Dennis is on the set out of earshot when the latter gets the poop. Tom, therefore, transmits the information through his mike into the earphones Dennis is presently wearing loosely around his neck. The words come over loud and clear for all to hear on the bridge: "Memo from Gene Roddenberry to Bob Wise: 'Thank the cast for the suspenders, but they make my pants ride too high.' "

Everyone is aware that Gene wears his pants very low on his hips, and we all have a good laugh, including the man who just happens to be standing next to Dennis at the time: the great baggy-legged bird of the galaxy himself.

5:05 p.m.: I have been sitting on the soundstage wondering what has changed in my life since I started in this picture. I guess I am looking for something profound, something that will make this film experience memorable to me in a philosophical way. I want it to be there, but try as I might, I can't find it. I can't, in fact, find a change on a less significant level. Surely *something* is different as a result of this experience. Before I can search further, we are called to rehearse the tag.

I surmise quickly that the intention is to shoot a master. I have no lines in the tag and I am wondering whether that means they will not cut away to me. Bear in mind that this is not just any sequence; it's the last shot in the movie. I would very much like to be in it. The more I think about it, the more I am convinced that Chekov will be omitted. Robert Wise passes by as I stand near my console smiling sardonically to myself over this likely eventuality. He asks what it is I find amusing, and without thinking I express my dissatisfaction over the camera angle about to be employed. He doesn't quite hear me the first time and asks that I repeat myself. In the brief moment before I start again, I flash on the realization that I am recreating the very unpleasant circumstances of my first day on the movie when I complained to him about how I was being photographed. I have no place to go but forward, however, because he is definitely waiting for me to again say what's on my mind.

Even as the words are tumbling out, I am preparing myself for another devastatingly embarrassing moment when he once more tells me not to worry about those "actorish things." All these months trying to bounce back from that disastrous beginning, and now a day from the ending I have placed myself in the exact same jeopardy.

He waits a beat before replying (it is the beat my heart skips) and then says: "There's no reason you have to be at your station the whole time. We'll move you in toward the center of the frame, Walter."

That simply, that unemotionally, the subject has been dispatched. No histrionics, no big thing, except that now my search is over. I have, after all, found a difference, a change I was looking for.

WEDNESDAY, NOVEMBER 22

The party's over.

7:45 a.m.: I run into Leonard again in the makeup room. He is feeling a bit dragged out this morning. He had spent the early part of the previous evening working on a rewrite of his lines in the tag and then went to Harold Livingston's house to consult with him on the proposed changes. Mix the long hours of the day with the long hours of the evening and stir with a couple of gin and tonics and you have on a Wednesday morning at 7:45 a somewhat droopy-eared Vulcan.

Actually, I am rather impressed by Leonard's tenacity. Here we are after four months—four months, incidentally, not without turmoil, confusion, conflict, frustration, and fatigue—finally approaching the last pages of the story and breathing a deserved sigh of relief for our successful effort, and there is Leonard still trying to improve upon the product, still trying to make it better. It is an admirable trait, one that speaks of character and integrity and leads me to believe that even without Spock in his life, Mr. Nimoy would have found a way to become an exceptional success in our business.

9:01 a.m.: Would you believe another rewrite of the tag? "HL—11/20/78 (6:30 P.M.); 11/22/78 (8:30 A.M.)—REVISED." That's thirty-one minutes ago! Next, we will shoot the scene in Harold's office just as he finishes spinning the cartridge on his typewriter.

9:19 a.m.: I step onto the bridge and discover that for the first time we will be bathed in light. No shadows, no mood effects for this scene. Every rinky-dink, baby, junior, senior, and K-Ten lamp that can be used to advantage is posted on the bridge.

I find it curious that despite all the talk of shooting the tag and the fact that most of us will finish on the picture by the end of the day, the finality of this occasion only starts to come home to me when I see the bridge all lit up. I guess what I'm put in mind of is a movie theater when the lights start to go on. The fantasy is about to end, the harsh light of reality has begun to intrude.

9:30 a.m.: We start rehearsing this ultimate version of the tag:

SCOTT: We can have you back on Vulcan in four days, Mr. Spock.

SPOCK: Unnecessary, Mr. Scott, I have no business on Vulcan.

Those are Spock's *written* words, anyway. What Leonard dryly says instead is: "If Dr. McCoy is to remain aboard, my presence here is essential." It's a funny line. We all break up. Leonard doesn't crack a smile. This is the speech he was working on the night before in an effort to bring a lightness to the ending.

We rehearse the scene again and this time he says the speech as written. A third time, and he again incorporates his own words. Gene is present throughout but says nothing. I am waiting to see if there will be a confrontation between them.

We shoot the master and the line spoken is the original one. If there was a discussion between actor and producer concerning the choice, I have missed it.

11:11 a.m.: Everyone is discussing the rightful ownership of the actors' chairs. These are the tall collapsible chairs known to the public as "directors' chairs." Ours have leather seats and backs and have our names stitched on them. Bill, George, Jimmy, Majel, Nichelle, and I are all vocal in the desire to take them home with us. There is opposition, however, from Dick Rubin, the property master, and it doesn't look as if we will succeed.

It's not the chairs themselves that drive us to pursue the matter beyond his first, second, and third "No," but what they represent, a tangible piece of *Star Trek,* of this experience, a source of instant recall. I find it charming that Bill, whose life has been crowded with filmic experiences these last ten years, who will surely go on to do at least as much in the future, is as vociferous as the rest of us.

Despite our persistence, Dick says "No" a fourth time and we slink away mumbling under our collective breaths.

11:25 a.m.: This last week the cast has been signing pictures for the crew. The activity reaches fever pitch on this last day. I'm sure that if the crew had pictures of themselves available, many of the cast would ask for *their* autographs. Isn't love grand!

12:00 p.m.: George, Nichelle, and I are requested on Stage Ten to host the luncheon and . . . guess what? Yup, have our pictures taken by the omnipresent publicity department. I really don't begrudge John Rothwell and his crew their photographic record of every well-intentioned company festivity. If only the documentation of these celebrations was not limited to the studio. It is somehow difficult to fully enjoy the spontaneity of a moment captured on a glossy "eight-by-ten" whose bottom legend is stamped "Copyright MCMLXXVIII by Paramount Pictures Corp. All Rights Reserved."

I sit down to lunch with Leonard, Bill, and Gene. No sooner has the last of our hundred guests filled his plate and seated himself than Bill is on the rise going back for seconds. My heart is full. I feel like a Jewish mother. Eat, dahlink, eat, I say to myself joyfully.

"GOING FOR SECONDS, EH, BILL?" says Leonard at a volume that can't be ignored.

The good Captain responds by faking a trip and spilling what's left of his fried rice into Mr. Spock's lap. Leonard laughs uproariously, but I'm aghast. Grease stains are immediately apparent on the Vulcan's uniform. I shake my head and "tsk-tsk" over what the wardrobe people will say. In the very short journey of these few errant grains, I have gone from Jewish mother to puritan biddy. Gad, the complexity of the human psyche!

5:23 p.m.: The rest of the afternoon is spent shooting covering angles of the master: three-shots, two-shots, closeups. Routine stuff. Business as usual. It could be any day. And yet Nichelle, Majel, Jimmy, George, and I are working for the last time. The earth hasn't opened up. The sky hasn't fallen in. God is obviously busy washing out His socks.

Oh, yes, when they finally come to Mr. Spock's closeup, two versions are shot: one with the original line and one with Leonard's invention. Tune in Christmas 1979 to find out which one they keep.

6:00 p.m.: Whoops! Done and yet not done. The publicity department would like to take some new group shots and we're all coming back on Friday for a sitting. Definitely an anticlimax. At least they could have had the good grace to give us a clean exit. If all the world's a stage, somebody better start looking for a play doctor. Oh, well, Happy Thanksgiving, everybody.

FRIDAY, NOVEMBER 24

Curtain call.

7:45 a.m.: In the makeup room. Everyone comes in logy from the holiday meals. The consensus is that between the food and the drink, the actors are in no condition to rise this early and preen for the camera. One after the other we log our complaints all the while sink-ing deeper into the bog. We are definitely in danger of submerging completely as George documents his travails: "After the turkey I had a little white and then a little red and then some more white and then some more. . . ."

"Yes," says Bill, almost to himself, ". . . and that was only the *women;* then he started drinking!" Hooray for the redoubtable Captain; we are rescued from self-pity.

9:15 a.m.: Would you believe it? We're not quite through, after all. Nichelle has a pickup to do from an earlier sequence and Jimmy has an added scene in the engine room. These will be shot before we get into the photo session.

9:51 a.m.: While we're waiting I congratulate Leonard on getting his version of Spock's tag speech on film. His rejoinder is, "I guess it was a bit devilish of me trying it out in front of Gene so that he could hear the laugh it would get." *"Devilish"?* Despite the pointy ears, that is not a word I would have thought in Leonard's lexicon. I find his use of it delightful but totally incongruous with my image of him. Next he'll tell me about something "impish" he has done. Ye, gads! Give me another sixteen weeks on this picture and maybe I'll begin to know who these people really are I'm working with.

10:31 a.m.: They have finished with Nichelle's and Jimmy's stuff very quickly and we now convene on the bridge for the last time. I've just heard Tom Overton refer to this set as a sarcophagus and I understand his point. If energy never ceases to exist and is, theoretically, convertible into matter, then certainly a tangible part of all of us will be sealed inside the bridge when they turn the lock.

We are given our choice of uniform to wear for the session. I decide on the Class-A outfit that I wore at the beginning of the production. Sixteen weeks and four and a half pounds later, I'm wondering whether the seams of my costume will weather the assault.

11:25 a.m.: The session is over and I return to my dressing room. I'm back in my own clothes in minutes and ready to leave.

I stand outside the soundstage facing the heavy doors. I am tempted to go back inside and say good-bye to everyone one more time. I hesitate long enough to reconsider. Let it go, let it go, Walter. Get on with life. There has always been and there will always be vistas, goals, triumphs beyond *Star Trek*. Cut the cord. Break new ground. Steer in fresh waters.

I spin on my heel and head away toward my car, my head high. I'm feeling very "together," very much my own man. The past is forgotten, the future is bright. Look out, world, here I come!

And, anyway, there's always the sequel.

ABOUT THE AUTHOR

WALTER KOENIG is a graduate of Fieldston High School
in New York, U.C.L.A. and the Neighborhood Playhouse School of the Theatre.

During the course of an acting career on the stage and
in film spanning two decades, he has performed as a
Welsh psychopath, an Armenian grape picker, A French
Resistance fighter, an Arabian rock-and-roll singer, a
German immigrant, a Puerto Rican towel attendant, a
Southern deputy sheriff, a Catholic monk, a Jewish ref-
ugee, and a Nazi sergeant.

Despite rumors to the contrary, Mr. Koenig has never
suffered an identity crisis of major proportions and has
never, *never* been institutionalized.

Among his accomplishments is a critically unclaimed
feature motion picture that Walter wrote and produced
back in the Sixties. That oversight notwithstanding, the
picture might have had a longer run were it not for two
untoward events: during its initial screening in Dallas,
the projectionist suffered cardiac arrest; during its initial
screening in Des Moines, the theater manager was ar-
rested. There has never been even the shreddiest of
evidence that either occurrence was attributable to the
film itself.

Mr. Koenig has written for television and has au-
thored episodes of "The Class of '65" and "Family" as

well as "Land of the Lost" and the animated "Star Trek" series.

He has directed theatrical productions of *Becket, America Hurrah!,* and *Hotel Paradise* in Los Angeles and has taught acting and directing techniques at U.C.L.A., The Sherwood Oaks Experimental Film College, and the California School of Professional Psychology.

Mr. Koenig has never shipped out on a freighter, worked an oil rig, or had a wolf for a pet. He is, however, an expert on bubble-gum cards, comic-strip character pinback buttons, and obsessive-compulsive acts of psycho-neurotic regression.

He is married to actress Judy Levitt. They have two sympathetic children, Joshua Andrew and Danielle Beth.